Testimonials

"Steve Eastin's family and ours have done business together for the better part of the last decade. What started as a business relationship has now turned into a great friendship. Steve's friends and acquaintances know that he has had a highly successful career, not just in law enforcement, but as an entrepreneur, as well. However, the success of those things stems in large part from the heart that Steve has. His strong heart for the Lord, his family, his friends, and really for everyone around him. As long as I have known him, what speaks the loudest is his love for people, his strong character, and the integrity with which he approaches all his personal and business relationships. He has a true desire to positively impact everyone around him, and an even stronger desire to give back to the law enforcement community that he served with for so many years. I have no doubt he will do just that, and whoever gets a chance to be exposed to this information is going to be much better for it. Steve has an amazing story and has been through the fire in many ways throughout his life. As a battle-tested man, literally and metaphorically, there isn't anyone better to share those experiences with the world. There isn't anyone more qualified to help navigate the minefields of life than those who have already crossed it themselves."

—Lorenzo Roybal
International Speaker and Entrepreneur

As a kid, I had the privilege of knowing Steve's wife from the school I went to. As I grew into an adult, I was blessed in meeting Steve. And since then, I have been honored to call him one of my dearest friends, confidant, and advisor in many of life's struggles. Not growing up with a father in my life, I have turned towards strong male role models to help mold myself. And I can say without a doubt that my friend Steve has been one of the most influential ones. He has shown me in many ways what being a well-balanced man means. As he has explained to me so many times, his close relationship with God is the number one reason he has been able to overcome obstacles in his path. As our relationship has grown, I have come to trust him in a way on all aspects of my life, whether it be relationships, finances, or just the day to day concerns that one has. I have seen countless times that he is always willing to lend a hand to a complete stranger. His compassion towards people is almost unparalleled by anyone I have ever met! I am proud to say Steve is and will always be someone I want to have in my life."

—Chase Mathews
Self-Employed Entrepreneur

"Steve has a way of leaving an impact on everyone he interacts with, and I'm certain this will be true of his book. I met Steve when I was fifteen through the police explorer program. At that time, I had no idea that he would become a mentor, teammate, and a lifelong friend of mine. Steve led the explorer program by the example of his work ethics, accountability, leadership, and integrity. At the age of twenty, I had the opportunity to apply and test for our police department's Crisis Negotiation Team (CNT), a dream of mine. I was the youngest candidate to date. I was prepared for and successful in this position because of Steve's mentorship throughout the years. During my time on the CNT, I worked closely with Steve and a team of other skilled first responders. We were paged to calls and situations that most will never fully understand or see in their lifetime. I witnessed firsthand his impact on others, most of the time while they were experiencing the darkest moments of their own lives. Steve has unique mindfulness about him and has always carried himself with integrity and humility. Over the years, Steve maintained a servant attitude, always putting others first while being respectful, kind, and generous, regardless of the situation at hand. Steve has dedicated his life to helping others and has been a huge blessing in mine. Thank you, Eastin, for the years you've dedicated to selfless service."

—Jody King
Retired Communications Specialist
and Crisis Negotiator

My wife and I have known Steve Eastin for several years and have had the opportunity to see him excel in many different areas of life. We know him as our business partner, realtor, and a great friend. What stands out most about Steve is his hard work ethic, focus, and drive to be a servant leader to those in his life. Even with his past in law enforcement, Steve has always remained optimistic in all areas of life. He is self-motivated and because of that, an inspiration to those in his life."

—Mark and Sarah Wiebenga
Self-Employed Entrepreneurs

Backup after the Beat

YOU ARE NOT CRAZY

True tales of life on patrol
And the journey that follows retiring the badge

By Steve Eastin

Disclaimer

The author is not an expert in psychology. The book contains stories based on the author's true life experiences. No part of this book should be considered professional advice. Always seek the advice of a competent professional.

Warning

Some of the contents in this book are violent, disturbing, and may not be suitable for all readers. Readers are advised to use their own discretion before moving ahead. Reading this book can stir up various emotions or triggers. There are sections that will make you feel sad, angry, anxious, or even frustrated, but can also make you feel happy, hopeful, or even relieved.

Contents

Acknowledgments

A SPECIAL THANK YOU to God and all the men and women who serve or who have served as first responders and to the families who have supported them along the way in their chosen profession.

I'd also like to thank everyone who helped in the completion of this book, which includes the department and town I served, testimonial providers, people who contributed their perspectives, editors, photographer, resources, and to those who have lived through this journey with us.

I thank my wife for never giving up on me and sticking with me no matter what I threw at her.

Thank you to my family and friends for always supporting me, even during my worst times. I'd like to thank my daughter, son, and son-in-law for always being my backup before and after the beat, and inspiring me to go on and want to leave a legacy, not of wealth but character.

Finally, I'd like to thank Vinil Ramdev and his company, Publishedge, for helping us produce a brilliant book.

Foreword

B EFORE I INTRODUCE myself, there is a part of me I need to share. At times, I may be extraordinarily blunt and candid. I don't screw around with words that have flowers and butterflies in them. If I say it, I mean it. No need to question my intentions because I will lay it all in front of you. That being said, the author behind this book, Steve, is an incredible man. I had the honor of working with him for many years. Being a street cop, Steve was genuine, both inside and out. He would give you the shirt off his back without you even asking for it. I can tell you about call after call where Steve would contact individuals or families who had no resources and found themselves homeless. Steve would personally take them to a local hotel, pay for their stay, and leave them with resources to help them get back on their feet again.

But don't get me wrong: I wouldn't screw with Steve. When shit hits the fan on a call, you better cooperate because you will not be getting any leniency. Steve meant business when it came to upholding the law and the safety of his officers, and he never tolerated it when a caller was disrespectful to dispatch.

Now, let me introduce myself: My name is Melissa O'Neill Varela. I come from a super-long line of law enforcement officers, all of whom worked for the Denver Police Department.

My grandfather, my dad, my mom, my brother, my uncle, and my cousin, and I know this will be a shock, but my husband is a police officer with another department. Law enforcement is in my blood. It's all I know. In my forty-four years, I have never had a normal holiday. I have eaten many cold dinners, and as a child, I would wake up numerous times in the morning, and my dad would be gone. It was not uncommon for him to be called out in the middle of the night. That was just the life of being the daughter in a law enforcement family. Little did I know then that my family would be living the same way. It seemed normal. What never came easy was seeing a breaking news story of an officer either shot or killed in the line of duty. I clearly remember several times when my life stood still, and everything around me stopped. You always pray it is not your loved one, and until you find out, you are temporarily paralyzed. I know a lot of you reading this know exactly what I am talking about. Once I knew my family was safe, my heart would instantly break for the family who had to experience this type of tragedy. It happens way too often that heroes are laying their lives down for you and me. As law enforcement, we unselfishly give to the community, our dads, husbands, wives, partners, and cousins. The list goes on and on. We trust that they will come home at night. This profession is their calling, and we believe they know what they have chosen.

I always knew I wanted to be a police officer. After obtaining my Associate's Degree in Criminal Justice, I decided to take the leap into law enforcement. I knew I was not ready to make a solid career decision yet, but I took the first step and was hired as a police dispatcher in a beautiful town with a population of around 19,000 people. I will never forget my first few nights on the job.

In 1999, at the young age of twenty-three, my first shift was nice and quiet. I worked with my training officer to learn the in's and out's of dispatch. Overwhelming? Absolutely! You literally have people's lives in your hands, and your decision-making abilities will not only impact the caller's fate but your officers' safety as well.

On top of that, there was a code for everything, and I could not understand any of the radio traffic. I found this to be extremely common for new dispatchers. I was lucky; I went through training before technology took off. I trained on a regular telephone with a switchboard in front of me, very old-school. I was exhausted by the time my shift was over. I had just completed my first graveyard shift from 9 p.m. to 7 a.m.

My second night, I was super excited. At this point, I had a good night's rest and was ready to take every 911 call that came in. Training was approximately twelve weeks long, and you would never be allowed to take a 911 call until you were at least four weeks into the training process. Also, your trainer would be right next to you listening-in, and they could take over the call immediately if needed. Nope, not me. I was ready tonight. I strutted in at 9 p.m. like I owned the place, wearing brand new jeans and my roommate's shirt.

My roommate had firmly told me I could not wear her new shirt, but I snuck it out of her closet and wore it anyway. I sat through the meeting, wondering what the officers were even talking about. It was like another language. I wondered if I might be in a little over my head and should maybe wait until the next day to be the star trainee and take all the 911 calls. I walked out of the meeting feeling defeated and walked towards dispatch when an officer yelled my name. I thought to myself, "Wow! He already knows me; I must be a big deal already." I flipped my hair, turned around to look at him, and said, "Yes?" He smiled and said, "21.99." I wondered if he was speaking in code again. I gave him a half-smile and continued towards dispatch, when I heard him yell, "You forgot to take the price tags off your jeans!" OMG, he was right. I had gone through an entire two-hour meeting and was introduced to the entire department with the price tags on my jeans that said $21.99 all the way down the front-right pant leg. I had no response. I went bright red. In a panic, I looked for the closest exit. Thoughts such as "I have to quit," "OMG, my life is over," and "I can never show my face in this town again," were racing through my mind. I should have known right then and there that it was going to be a horrible night.

After running into the only bathroom in the PD, I took the tags off my jeans, said a couple of cuss words, and tried to regain my composure so I could start my shift. Deciding not to quit, I tiptoed into dispatch, where my trainer was waiting and dropped my huge training binder on the table. I took a deep breath and thought I was ready to start my shift. But boy, was I wrong...

At about 3 a.m., I was reading my training manual and looked up to see one of my officers standing near me right next to the fax machine. At the same time, I heard a loud bang. I thought to myself, "OMG! He dropped the fax machine." The officer suddenly hit the ground and my trainer yelled at me to get down. I remember thinking to myself, "I'm not falling for this." My trainer yelled again for me to get down. I hesitantly got under my desk, so they wouldn't think I was falling for the joke. Suddenly, multiple shots rang out, and the window in front of me was blown out as rounds kept coming in. My trainer was under her desk on the phone, asking another agency for help. I remember thinking to myself, "That's it. I am really quitting this time." I was in a small enclosed room, and there was only one way out, and I could not safely get to the door. I froze and just laid down on the floor, thinking I was going to die. I thought a lot about my parents and how thankful I was for them, and then I thought to myself, "Shit, I am going to die in my roommate's shirt," and then I found an inner peace I had never felt before. I just laid there and waited to die. We were all trapped and could not make it to the door.

I could hear multiple officers screaming at the suspect. I had no idea what was going on. Then it suddenly stopped, and there was an eerie kind of quiet. I remember looking up and seeing a man dead on the street, with a gun next to him. The next thing I heard on the police radio was that there were dead children in his vehicle, which was parked outside the PD. It turned out that this awful person had killed his kids. So he wanted the police to kill him. I learned a new term that night: "Suicide by Cop."

I remember calling my dad and telling him that I was quitting, and he had to come and get me then and there. My truck was part of the crime scene as it was parked near the location of the shooting, so I was not allowed to touch it. While waiting, our police chief showed up and came into dispatch. He pointed to the bullet holes in a file cabinet and said, "Look how close this round was to you and your trainer." I remember feeling lightheaded, and he grabbed me by the shoulder and sat me down. Once my parents showed up, I could not get out of there quick enough. I remember walking to the car and noticed that my parents had been to a McDonald's drive-through to grab breakfast on their way to get me.

I could not believe it. I had almost died, and they went to McDonald's first! It's funny . . . the little things you remember. For the next two days, I was okay and slept well. I thought to myself, "Wow, you're taking this really well." But suddenly, out of nowhere, I started crying uncontrollably. I could not sleep. I felt numb. After five weeks off, I went back. Yes! I returned to the room in which I almost died and picked right back up where we left off in the training process. To this day, the only issue I have is a phobia of windows. Apparently, the suspect had sat outside and watched my trainer and me through the window before he started shooting!

Even now, twenty years later, I will not sit by a window if the blinds are open and it is dark outside. I look back now and thank God I did not know the officers involved the way I do today, as that would have been a game-changer. I was very resilient back then since I was single with no kids, and honestly, I still had to use a map to get to work. I was so new. One of my best friends is buried a couple of headstones over from the kids who were murdered. I stop by yearly and bring them flowers.

Thankfully, things started to slow down. I began to get to know everyone at the police department, and in 2000 we moved to a brand-new building . . . thank God! It was nice not to be in that room anymore. I graduated from training and was on my own, meaning that I could answer 911 calls all by myself. The first few years of being a dispatcher, things were mostly slow—we did not take a lot of phone calls for police assistance. We were still a tiny town. But I loved all my co-workers, and I loved my job. And guess what? There were multiple windows that surrounded us in dispatch, and my co-workers will tell you that, as soon as it started to get dark, I would be the first one to shut all the blinds. I did that every shift for the next nineteen years.

As our calls for service started to increase, we started taking more serious calls. During this time, I was shocked to realize how citizens calling in for help often lie to the dispatcher. I will never forget taking a domestic violence call in which the male caller convinced me that his wife had hit him several times, and that she went downstairs. My job was to make sure he was safe and that my officers were safe once they arrived on scene. I was so empathetic to him and his situation. Once my officers arrived on scene, they found his wife on the couch unconscious. He had choked her to an unconscious state and left her there to go and call 911. "What? No, that's not what happened—he told me she'd hit him! Wait. Did he lie?" I thought to myself. Yes, that happens a lot, and I fell for it. Wow! I felt so stupid. How did I not realize it? I should have asked to speak with her. I asked myself if I was cut out for the job. What if she had died? Would I have saved her? I quickly learned that these types of thoughts go racing through a dispatcher's head regularly because, in that job, you always think you could have done more.

As my career went on, I became a trainer myself. I trained many people to become the best dispatchers they could possibly be. I also learned a good lesson as a trainer: not everyone is meant to do this job, and not everyone wants to be the best at this job. We had a high turnover rate with new dispatchers in training. A lot of new hires came into this job as though they could do it with their eyes shut. They had no idea the multi-tasking it takes to do it successfully. Not only must you listen to the caller, but you must also be aware of what officers are saying on the radio, and what your partner needs from you pertaining to something completely different. There are also multiple phone lines ringing that are your responsibility to answer, requiring you to prioritize which calls need your urgent attention. At the same time, you have officers coming in and out of dispatch needing something.

Did I mention there is a phone for walk-in citizens in the vestibule of the PD that goes directly to dispatch? Well, those calls are also your responsibility. If shit hits the fan on the police radio, all non-emergency calls are put on hold, and your job is to help your partner with crazy radio traffic. While you're doing that, you must also answer incoming 911 calls and put a call in for service that has nothing to do with the crazy radio traffic. Then, someone requests the fire department over the radio. That is just a small glimpse of the kind of multi-tasking dispatchers do every shift. Some people can do it and some people can't. I have found that a number of new hires had no idea what they were getting themselves into when they took the job. That is why I say it's a calling. Being a police dispatcher pays well, and we have great insurance. But I've also found new dispatchers who think they're going to make great money. But the first suicide call they take in training is often also their last day. Many cannot make it through some of the brutal calls for service we receive, no matter how well it pays. Regardless of all of this, I loved being a trainer. I had a great partner and the privilege of working with the best team of talented dispatchers.

As partners, you each begin to learn each other's styles, each other's strengths and weaknesses, and you pick up each other's slack without being asked. You know they have your back and you have theirs.

Your fellow dispatchers became your family. I took some awful calls: calls I never wish to share again. At such times, my fellow partners and co-workers would be by my side in a heartbeat. There is absolutely nothing you will not do for each other as a result of having worked in a room together daily for ten to twelve hours a shift. I cannot praise my team enough. I constantly learned from them. I relied on them. They made life or death decisions in seconds. Speaking from experience: if you make a mistake, you will never make it again, and no one will be harder on you about it than yourself. To this day, I am constantly told that I am too hard on myself—it sticks with you even after the job.

I will never forget one call I took. It was from a woman calling from her home saying that her husband had grabbed a shotgun after they'd argued, and he was going to kill her. He was intoxicated on the couch while she was on the phone with me. Due to the severity of the call, I could only ask her "yes or no" questions because her husband couldn't know she was on the phone with 911. Things started to escalate while we were talking. I asked her if he was pointing the gun at her. She said, "Yes!" In those two seconds, I had to make a decision about what she should do. I thought to myself: she could stand there and possibly get shot; or she could run. Either way, the outcome would be bad. Thank God, I already had officers in the area. I remember saying her name in a very calm voice, then I said, "I'm going to count to three. At three, you are going to run as fast as you can out the front door. Do you understand?" So, I counted to three, closed my eyes, and yelled, "Run!" That was the longest five seconds of my life; I knew I was either going to hear my officers state they had visual on her coming out the front door, or I was going to hear a gunshot. Thankfully, she made it out to my officers safely. I knew this was a fortunate outcome that rested solely on my quick decision. These are the things you must live with as a police dispatcher.

I remember one of my former bosses telling me during one of my yearly evaluations that I was too quiet. For those who know me, I swear she really said that. She said I needed to work on my communication skills, stand up for myself more, and not be afraid to give my opinion. Wow, if she had only known what was to come. In 2003, I was selected to be on our ERT Team (Emergency Response Team). It's like a SWAT team, but our department called it ERT. I was chosen to be a scribe on the team. Being a scribe, I was to go to all the prominent callouts: barricaded subjects; suicidal parties; shooting suspects; suspects holding hostages, and so on. I made a log of the entire call.

For example, I would write down threats/demands, suspect information, etc. I was on cloud nine. Then, I was asked to cross-train as a hostage negotiator. What? Does this mean I get to talk to the hostage-taker on the phone? Yes! But then came the doubts: can I do this? What if I screw up? What if they shoot someone? What if the suspect doesn't listen to me? Wait! Didn't my former boss just get done telling me that I needed to work on my communications skills? Is this what she was talking about? As a hostage negotiator? I mean, aren't we jumping the gun a little here? I thought we could take baby steps, but what the heck! Let's do it! Boy, I had no idea the amount of training that would go into my new role. In my seventeen years as a negotiator, I completed hundreds of hours of training. My ERT negotiators became my family, and I had the opportunity to work with Steve on several callouts. Let me tell you, he is a natural.

The way he can de-escalate a situation is unbelievable. I can say, as both police dispatcher and negotiator, I learned more from watching others do it, and it became an invaluable experience.

In 2010, our ERT team was disbanded. It was a heart-breaking moment. Those were some of the best days of my career. The brass decided to move into a regional team, so four of the best police agencies came together to form a Regional SWAT Team and Negotiations Team. I knew deep down I really wanted to be on the new team, but I was nervous about trying out as I knew I would be up against the best. But I worked hard and put together my resume; this was followed by oral boards, a written test, and a mock negotiation. Several days later, I found that I had made the team. I could not believe it. I was so excited, but I knew it was not going to be an easy task. I trained with some of the best negotiators in the country, and again, my new team became my family. There is nothing in the world I would not do for them. We knew each other so well; and if things went south on a call, we not only hurt together but we also laughed together. Those times were truly some of the best moments of my career.

Soon, we changed our team name to CNT—the Crisis Negotiations Team. In 2015, I was asked to be the team leader for our CNT team. What an honor it was not only being able to work with the best but having the trust of the team about my decisions as their leader. I could tell you a million stories about our callouts, but there is one that really touched me personally. It was during a bitterly cold fall day in the late afternoon. Our team received a call involving a suicidal male armed with a gun who had received some bad news from his doctor. My sergeant asked me to be the primary negotiator; and we went in the bearcat, which is a tank filled with SWAT members and is pretty much indestructible. We drove up to the front of the house.

Sure enough, we finally saw a man with a gun to his chest. Sometimes during these types of calls, you find a connection with the person on the other side. I could only talk to him through a loudspeaker, and I was unable to hear his responses. At moments like that, you rely on your training and your teammates. You have your entire team backing you up and feeding you information even though they're not there with you. I talked to the man for a while, watching him put the gun down, pick it back up, then back down again, repeatedly. I kept encouraging him, telling him that he had so much to live for and that we just needed to sit down and sort things out. After about an hour or so, I felt comfortable asking him to put the gun down and make his way to the door. At that point, my number one priority was the safety of my SWAT team, so I had to make sure he came out peacefully. It was like watching in slow motion, as he finally put the gun down, walked to the door, and came out. That was the first time I had the chance to talk to a subject face to face. I remember him looking at me and saying, "I just wanted to die." I looked back at him and said, "Not today." I truly believed that he had so much to live for but was having a bad day. Sometimes our minds get into such a fog that we are not able to see our true reality. Sometimes our bodies go into shock with news that we cannot process. I strongly feel this is what happened in this situation. Throughout my career, we would come across good people who were simply lost and didn't know how to pick themselves back up. That call will always stay with me; I will never forget his face and the emotions around his coming out. Our CNT unit was used to being cussed at by suspects, being called every name in the book, and our families and us being put down. Suspects would try anything to get a rise out of us, but it didn't work. Over time, we became resilient to this type of behavior and came to expect it. So, having said all that, you can tell that I was no longer the quiet person afraid to share my opinion. There's no doubt being a negotiator changed me. Over the years, I built up a strong personality, voiced my opinion often, and never held back if I had something to say. I think talking with horrible, violent criminals changes you. You must wear a suit of armor to deflect all the negativity.

Not every call turned out in our favor, and there were plenty of "what if's?" But one thing never changed—we were always there for each other and never stopped supporting our mission together as a team.

Man, what I would give to go back to those days. Every single day since 2018, I have missed my dispatch team, my patrol team, and all the wonderful people I had worked with. I miss my negotiations team. There are no words to explain the magnitude of what they have all meant to me over the last twenty years. I have tears in my eyes as I write this. No matter what, they will always be a part of me.

In 2017, our CNT team was called out to a barricaded subject armed to the teeth and possibly holding one of our deputies hostage. I was one of the CNT members who responded to the call. We did everything in our power to instill communication with the shooter, but it was obvious that a tactical solution was needed. We knew the suspect potentially had in his custody a deputy hostage, who was someone I knew personally and worked with. I knew he was alive and thought he would be okay. Tragically, the ending was not what I expected. The shooter killed my deputy trapped inside, and several other deputies were shot but recovered. The shooter was killed.

After that callout, I went straight to work and worked four twelve-hour shifts in dispatch. Talk about a blur. It is hard to recall what happened during these four days. I was so lucky to have such a fantastic dispatch partner. She is genuinely one of the best, and I don't say that lightly. Together we mourned the death of the slain deputy. We were all mourning one of our own, as he had worked for our department before taking a job with our neighboring sheriff's department. We also had so many unanswered questions about what happened. Even though I was on scene when our deputy was killed, I still did not know what actually took place. Over that four-day period, I heard lots of different stories about it from my officers. If you're a dispatch team leader or supervisor, one bit of solid advice I can give you is to get your dispatchers and civilian staff to do a debriefing after a major incident like this one. No excuses! I will talk more about that in a bit.

Here is where it gets raw and real: Several weeks after the shooting, I started having intense jaw pain. Next thing I knew, my jaw was locked closed. I knew it wasn't TMJ (Temporomandibular

Joint Disease, which affects the joints of the jaw through damage or degeneration) because this was a completely different type of pain. It was debilitating, and I had no idea what was wrong with me. I went to my local dentist, and he tried everything to ease the pain. He tried to unlock my jaw and realign my teeth as my bite was entirely off. With no success, he sent me to physical therapy. After several months of physical therapy, my pain was increasing. I was starting to lose weight and doing my job became harder. Several of my officers said I was slurring over the radio, which was true. With my jaw being locked, I could not open my mouth far enough to talk. I still had no idea what was going on and had never experienced this type of pain. Then, the nightmares came on. They were horrific. I was afraid to go to sleep because I did not want to see the horrible images in my head. I started having anxiety; I would come home after work and sit in my car before going inside and just cry. Why was I feeling like this? What was wrong with me? I was exhausted and in pain. Only one thing stood clear and true—I loved my job. It was my passion and I looked forward to going to work.

In June of 2018, after about six months of suffering these symptoms with no relief in my jaw and losing around ten pounds, I continued to work. Then it all came to an unexpected head. As I was leaving to work, the last thing I remembered was opening the door to the garage to get in my car. The next thing I know, I was on the cement floor of the garage where my sweet nine-year-old daughter found me. She went to get my husband, who took me to the ER. I remember texting my partner and telling her I was going to be late.

Once we arrived at the emergency room, I learned that I had passed out, fallen down the garage stairs, and landed on the floor. It was due to exhaustion and lack of nutrients. Luckily, other than that, I was physically fine, with no broken bones. I remember telling the doctor how much my jaw hurt and how I had been unable to be on a normal diet for months. The ER doctor asked me if I had suffered any recent trauma. I mentioned the shooting and the nightmares, which I considered irrelevant. I was ordered to rest for the next couple of days and drink protein shakes, as my body was being deprived of nutrients.

I started to slowly piece the puzzle together; and with my family's help, I realized that I had never adequately processed the shooting, and these were all side effects of pushing the events of the shooting deep down to where no one could see them . . . not even me.

A couple of days later, I went to see a doctor. She told me that I was showing all the signs of PTSD and exhaustion, and that I needed to be taken out of work. I remember telling her repeatedly that I was fine. All I wanted to do was go back to work. I kept asking how long I was going to be out and was told that it would depend on my progress. Progress? What progress? I was totally fine!

The jaw pain continued for months. Soon, I had lost twenty pounds and ended up going to my childhood dentist. I was desperate for answers and just wanted to go back to work. I saw him about two or three times a week. He knew me well as I had been his patient for over twenty years. He tried everything he could think of to ease my jaw pain, with no luck. After doing an MRI, he told me my jaw was in bad shape—so bad that he referred me to an oral surgeon.

During this time, I also sought counseling and tried to figure out what this PTSD thing was all about and why I was having such bad nightmares. I had successfully been a police dispatcher for years. How could this be happening to me? Where did I go wrong? I taught classes to new hires and other departments, emphasizing how important it was to take care of yourself both mentally and physically (as being a dispatcher can be rough at times). I was the expert on this! How did I miss all the signs?

Well, I can tell you that after eight surgeries on my face, I still missed the signs. I have now been diagnosed and accepted the fact that I have PTSD. During my extreme nightmares after the shooting, I would grind my teeth and had torn my TMJ to pieces. I had a full joint replacement on the left side of my face, with a prosthetic joint and titanium plates. I have lost some movement in my face, which is permanent.

I have put in countless hours of physical therapy and speech therapy to learn how to smile again and wake up my facial muscles. I also meet with my nutritionist, who had helped me with my liquid diet for the last two years, helping me move up to a soft diet. I continued to lose more weight. Being five foot ten, I only weighed one hundred and five pounds. She continues to help me with weight gain and getting all the proper nutrients with my limited chewing capabilities. A year later, I still slur my words and continue to have daily facial pain. My nightmares have not stopped to this day despite intense counseling. I recently found out that I am soon to undergo a full joint replacement on my right TMJ. It is hard to think I have to go through the same thing all over again. But if I have learned anything, it is that I am stronger than anything put in front of me.

While going through all this, I lost myself; I lost my identity; and I had some extremely dark days. I put my family and friends through hell. At times, they did not know how to help me. I didn't know how to help myself. I couldn't see the light at the end of the tunnel. At the end of 2019, when I thought I could not take it anymore more, it happened—I lost my job. I have still not completed all my medical treatment that would have enabled me to be released back to work. The department could no longer hold my position. That was the final hit. I felt overwhelmed with grief. Everything I loved—my passion, my career, my co-workers—all gone! My negotiations career, gone. I entered a dark stage of mourning, which was extremely rough. To this day, I still struggle with it a lot. I miss my teammates. I miss my career.

So, back to the debriefing. I had never attended a debriefing after the shooting. I remember one opportunity I had to attend but it was during my shift, so I was unable to go. I had created a story and dialogue in my head of what happened that awful day. I created it after listening to my co-workers speculate about what happened day in and day out. We were all trying to figure out this dreadful tragedy. As the stories went on, I started living in a false reality, where I blamed myself for my deputy's death. Based on the stories I had heard, I felt I had let my CNT team down. I should have done more. If I had done my job differently, he would still be alive. Now, that's a lot to put on yourself. It turns out that these stories I created were not based on facts, as there was nothing I could have done differently. Only over two years later did I have my first debrief on the shooting. It was tough to listen to but extremely beneficial. I realized the story I had created in my head never happened, and I was finally able to replace it with the truth. If I had just known the facts from the beginning, this never would have happened to me. If I had just gone to one debrief, I would have known the facts. I would still have my job. I would not have a prosthetic joint, with another one to follow. I would not have PTSD. Really? Absolutely not! It's easy to think like that and blame others, but you must learn to accept the cards you are dealt with, or you will never begin to heal. There is no one to blame, no one to point a finger at. This is my life, and I accept every single day of it. I would rather lose my job by doing my job. In the end, I would do it all over again if it meant keeping every single one of my officers safe. It's not my job ... it's my calling.

If I had one mission in life, it would be that every dispatcher and civilian staff member is included in a debriefing after a critical incident. It's truly invaluable. The importance of a debrief did not hit me until a year or so later because I thought all the events, as I had heard them, were true and that I was okay. No! I was not okay. Two years was a long time to wait for my first debrief, and I stumbled into the debriefing by accident. It was not a planned debrief of which I was aware, so you can imagine my shock. After the presentation was over, I had the opportunity to ask the presenter several questions about the shooting, just the two of us. He sat there for an hour and listened to me ask question after question about what had happened that day. He had been right in the middle of everything, so he was able to answer all my questions. I got my life back that day. It gave me my first breath of freedom, my first breath of life again, and my first breath of being able to feel again. It freed me from the horrible nightmare in which I had been trapped for so long.

Now, in 2020, I want to share with you what I have learned from my journey in order to illustrate that things do get easier. I have found my passion and my purpose. The flame inside me that was blown out is back and shining brighter than ever. I never thought I would feel that again. I had to experience the pain with full force, both mentally and physically, to find the purpose of my journey. It would be selfish to have lived through it and not share the story. I hope one person reading this will be reassured that there is always a light at the end of the tunnel. Don't ever give up on yourself. Take it one day at a time. Don't waste your strength on yesterday or tomorrow. Use your strength for today. The "whys," "whats," and ifs" will kill you. Never go down that road. Sometimes, you must walk the entire path to find the answers. I know I have unbelievable strength, and I will never give up on this fight. I have a great team of doctors who have shown me that PTSD is real. I am so thankful for my family and for my support group of friends who continue to support me daily. I am grateful for my religion and faith. I could not have done any of this without God being front and center in my life. Ten percent of me died on the day of the shooting and throughout my journey. But I have learned that you can go harder and stronger at ninety percent than you ever could at a hundred!

Let's get real here for a minute. The last two years of my life have been a walking nightmare from which I could not wake up. At one point, I was so malnourished and underweight that the doctor had "the talk" with me. He explained that I was not going to survive if I did not get the proper nutrients into my body as soon as possible. I was admitted to the hospital overnight. On top of that, I had still not accepted that I had PTSD. All I did was cry. Those were the darkest days of my life. But I kept reminding myself, "You are not a quitter; you don't know how to quit." I woke up one day and said to myself, "I am done! I am ready to fight back." I picked myself up off the ground for the hundredth time and started doing the work.

During counseling, I faced the demons that were haunting me every day. I worked my ass off in counseling and faced every single emotion I had not dealt with. I did a ton of research on PTSD and finally admitted to myself that I have it. I continue to work with my counselor every week. As many of you know, it is properly called PTSI (Post Traumatic Stress Injury). I came to the hard conclusion that my life as I knew it was gone. The old

Melissa no longer existed. But I became so excited to meet the new Melissa. That meant discovering who I had become after this life-changing injury. I started to look towards the future and wondered what my new life was going to look like, the prospect of which excited me. I put lots of energy into creating a healthy mindset. I opened the door and kicked out all those dark moments. They were no longer welcome, including those telling me that people were going to judge me or look at me differently for having PTSD. Nope, that hasn't happened.

I love all my doctors. Physical therapy and speech therapy have played a huge role in my recovery. But what has really changed is my mindset. You know you are doing better when you walk into your eighth surgery holding your head high and saying, "Let's do this." I now study nutrition, and I hate nutrition books! But boy, have I educated myself on what goes into my body, and I now understand why certain nutrients are vital to my health. In addition to this, I love fitness. I can also tell you everything you want to know about PTSD. I love studying the mind, and how to create and maintain a healthy mind. I also love hearing from survivors of PTSD who almost gave up, but instead are glad they decided to give life another chance. Wow, they motivate me like there is no tomorrow!

But here is where it gets tricky. Let me give you a little of the behind-the-scenes that played into this story. Steve approached me about writing my story for this book. I felt honored that he had asked me when he had a million other people to choose from. I was so excited but told him I would have to think about it. I started to have a little anxiety about it. It just didn't feel right. After everything I just told you about finally loving my life again, I couldn't manage to talk about the day that changed all our lives. I became overwhelmed. I called Steve and told him I was sorry, but I couldn't do it. I wasn't ready. But I have always been harder on myself than anyone could ever be, and the thoughts started running through my head: "You are not a quitter," "How will you ever know your strength if you don't at least try?" Ugh! Why could I not talk about it? It turns out I could! I just had to remind myself that I have the strength to do anything. So, I opened my computer and started writing. I laughed through parts of it, but once I began to write about the calls and my co-workers, I started to cry and stopped typing. It was getting too hard. I was reminded again that I am no longer a police dispatcher; that passion was gone from my life, and I miss it. I miss my team. But I pulled myself together and carried on. When I hit the paragraph about the shooting was when things got a little rough. My mind is still processing the real story. I had another story ingrained in my mind for two years that never happened. It had only been two months since I learned the truth about what had truly unfolded. So, it was going to take a bit of time for my mind to transition into the real story and let the emotions around the old story dissipate. Complicated, I know! But I had instant relief after the debrief.

As I continued writing, I came to the part I was dreading the most: the shooting. Once again, I had to stop. I just couldn't type the words anymore, so I skipped over the paragraph altogether and left it blank. I went right into writing about my jaw injury. But that empty paragraph just stared at me. It had been two years, and I still couldn't write about it? What was wrong with me? I eventually did write about it, but not without help from my counselor. I was more frustrated with myself that it had been so long and that I was still having an adverse reaction dealing with it. It seems crazy, but it is also natural and okay.

Occasionally, I have to go easy on myself. I am awaiting another major surgery on my face. I am still recovering from my eighth surgery; I am working through my nightmares; I am still processing the grief of losing my job; and I am working through the PTSD. Oh, did I mention the fact that I am a mom to beautiful triplets? It's a lot to take all of this on at once! So, it's okay not to be okay all the time. I will have triggers here and there, but I have learned techniques and have tools to work through them now. I still have very graphic nightmares every single night. My doctors and I are still working on them, and I will conquer them. But in the meantime, I wake up exhausted every morning. I have learned how to shake it off and not let it interfere with my duties as a wife and a mom. The PTSD no longer controls me. I control it. There will always be bad days, like the one I just shared, but I also have many more good days. The best thing I ever did was reach out and ask for help. I have learned that I am not alone. I have had countless people tell me about their battle with PTSD, and their stories sound very familiar. I have met people who have been suicidal because the racing thoughts never end. PTSD can be brutal, but it does get easier with the right counseling, the right mindset, the right doctors, the proper education, and the right support system.

I believe one of the most important things you can do is educate yourself and your family and friends about PTSD and what to expect. My husband had no idea what to do. He had to learn. He had to educate himself about PTSD, its effects, and how to support me through the hard times, especially in the beginning. Now, he has such a deep understanding that he can educate and help others because he has been through it. Even though you will always have triggers, you will learn all the tools to work through them, and they will become second nature. You must stay in the fight. You have a great life ahead of you, so suicide is never the answer. This will pass. It will leave a battle scar on you; you will always have reminders, but you will learn everything you need to live an extremely happy life. But first, you must ask for help. That is the hardest step in the process, but it will also be the best thing you will ever do for yourself. Remember, you are stronger than any obstacle that could ever be put in front of you.

People think there is a stigma in asking for help, especially with PTSD symptoms. I bet you all can tell me what that stigma is. Yep, that you will lose your job! Yes! This happened in my case, but my agency held my position for eighteen months. When they saw no end in sight, and with multiple surgeries still ahead, they had to let me go. It was only fair that my position was filled, which allowed dispatch to be up to full strength. It is still tough for me to accept this, and I have my good and bad days, but I do not want this to deter you from asking for help. Police and fire agencies across the nation now have phenomenal mental health and wellness programs set up for this exact reason. I was out longer due to the extent of my facial injuries. You will not be treated differently or looked at differently if you have PTSD. It doesn't define you. It just becomes a part of you, and you should be proud of yourself for taking steps to get help. It is not easy, but well worth it!

Steve will never know how grateful I am to him. He pushed me way out of my comfort zone on this one. But I also accomplished something therapeutically by writing my story. I know I will continue to work on "hot spots" that come up during my recovery, just as they did while writing this story. But how will you know what those are if you do not give yourself a chance to identify and fight them? I can only hope that my story will change the life of at least one person reading this because you were my drive.

BEST WISHES,

MELISSA O'NEILL VARELA

Dedication

THIS BOOK IS dedicated to the following men and women: all those who are active or retired in law enforcement; dispatchers; military; fire personnel; correction officers; emergency medical service workers; and civilian employees such as victim's advocates, record clerks, court employees; and the various types of first responders. It is dedicated to all those who wake up each day and kiss their families goodbye, knowing that it could be their last day, but not letting that stop them from performing their duties to protect and serve their country and respective communities. This includes families that support these brave folks in their chosen professions.

"But the Lord is faithful, and He will strengthen you and protect you from the evil one."[1]

I also dedicate this book to my parents, who raised me to know the difference between good and evil, and between right and wrong; to respect and understand authority; and to fight for the defenseless. My parents taught me to love and give unconditionally, stick together no matter what, and fight for one another; to dream big, and never quit anything you begin

---

[1]   2 Thessalonians 3:3 NIV

or believe in. They also taught me that if you are surrounded by evil, negative, and selfish people, that you should find new people (not because you don't care, but because they don't). My parents were, and always will be, the foundation of my life.

The inspiration behind this book is to let every person who has served their community as a law enforcement officer or a first responder to know that most of the world holds a high level of respect for them. Also, that there are people like me who will continually fight to change the attitude and hearts of the haters.

My Prayer

M Y PRAYER IS that this book will reach millions of people and open their eyes to the daily lives of first responders and law enforcement officers and show how they deal with their lives along the way. If you are someone bearing hatred towards law enforcement officers or first responders, I pray that this book will persuade you to have a healthier and more positive attitude toward people in these professions.

Yeah, I see 'enough is enough' posted everywhere, but what are we really doing? More specifically, what am I doing? I am sharing my story in an attempt to improve the lives of those who are fighting the fight.

I'll be sharing most of my life story with you and tell you about my experiences serving as a police officer for more than eighteen years. I had the honor of working with all types of people. It did not matter to me what race, color, national origin, sex, religion, age, beliefs or what a person's sexual preference was. I did not care! All that I knew was that God chose this profession for me and that I swore an oath that I would serve and protect all people. I know this to be true as well with so many other first responders who took the same or similar oath. I believe that you should leave a person in a better place than how you found them.

This leads us to another reason for writing this book: to share with first responders what they may experience after leaving their profession. At the end of it all, are they both mentally and physically healthy? I have witnessed so many first responder retirees die shortly after they leave. So, if you are a first responder, don't let that be you.

I pray that you have plenty of love and support while working the beat and after the beat.

CHAPTER 1

Behind the Why

A FTER I RETIRED from law enforcement in 2015, it took me approximately four years to muster the courage to share my experiences in writing. However, I did know that I would want to share my story someday. So, after I retired, I started taking notes. There have been several nights when I would lay on my bed and think about the prospect of this book. I cannot tell you how many times over the past four years I have jumped out of bed with a thought I needed to write down.

It wasn't really until 2019 that I felt the time was right. There were several deciding factors in writing this book: one being to share awareness and help new first responders prepare for their lives during their tour of duty and urge them to maintain a healthy lifestyle. This book also touches on life after the tour of duty—when it's important to continue living a healthy lifestyle. When their careers end, we can only pray that it was their choice, or that they've survived long enough to retire financially.

Some people can just shut it off and leave it all behind, but many can't figure out how to move past their tour of duty, memories, and experiences. I fell into the second category.

Readers of this book may fit into one of those categories, or they may not. They may not even know that they fit into one of those categories until after they have read this book. There are many stages to a first responder's career, and the category they fall into depends upon the stage they are currently at.

I hope to also attract those family members who may not know how to handle situations involving their loved ones, to attract those who have left the first responder field, or at least try to help them understand what the retiree might be going through. Trust me on this: the loved ones of first responders are with them, right in the thick of it.

Due to the violence in the world today and the negativity towards law enforcement and first responders, I believe with every fiber in my body that it's time to let the world know what these brave people, and their families, deal with on a daily basis. I'm adamant about getting this information to the eye of the public. The overall negative perception of police officers and other first responders must change. I will be sharing my experiences that took place during, and after, law enforcement duty; the challenges I faced; as well as how my family and I worked through all of them.

There have been a few choices in my life of which I am not proud, especially the ones where someone was hurt emotionally. Although there are few, I'm certain they know who they are. I'm genuinely sorry, and I pray for your forgiveness, as I have forgiven.

Though I may not go into detail regarding some of my few poor choices, I can guarantee you that my wife and I have discussed everything in my life, and we've decided to leave it in the past—which is where our poor choices belong. Can you relate? No offense, but I'm just being blunt here. Worry about your own sins, because God's going to be asking you about your sins, not mine.

Recently, during a conversation with my friend Melissa, I admitted to her that there were things in my past of which I was not so proud. This is how she responded:

"Steve, the things in our past build character and strength. If you stop and look, you will see your life lessons all over the place, but you can never live with the fear of regret. You use the past to better yourself and learn from it. You might not be proud of some of those things, but they have had a big impact on the inspiring person you are today."

That really sunk in, and I hope that it hits home with you as well.

2 Corinthians 6 in the Bible says that today is the day for salvation, no matter what you've done in your past. None of us are perfect![2]

I'm no psychology expert. But I will still be sharing a session with a licensed professional counselor based on her thoughts of my memories and experiences, and the traumatic effect they have had on my life. Hopefully, someone can relate. I hope this

---

[2] 2 Cor 6:2 NIV

information will make life a bit easier for first responders after being in the midst of everything and give them an understanding of what they and their families might face after they hang up the uniform.

There is no doubt that if it weren't for those people who dedicate their lives to saving their country and communities, the world would be in total chaos. People would face no consequences for their evil actions, and there would be no protection for our children and grandchildren from the many predators out in the world. First responders are willing to give their lives to protect the innocent and defenseless. So, tell me: doesn't that deserve some added recognition, gratitude, and respect?

I pray that anyone getting into the first responder profession reads this book and keeps it, so they can read it again after their term of duty has ended. Know this: there is always someone out there who is willing to help while you're serving. I also pray that whoever retires from the first responder profession knows that there's help available if they need it. This book will supply some resources and, hopefully, some understanding of what you may experience, either mentally or physically, after leaving the profession. During all the training classes I took, training me how to survive and take care of myself while on duty, there was never anything helpful about understanding and managing the potential negative after-effects of the service.

Unfortunately, the suicide and death rate for first responders is atrocious. In January 2020, *USA Today* published an article on a Massachusetts-based nonprofit organization called Blue

H.E.L.P., which is an organization that allows individuals and agencies to report active and retired officers' suicide deaths on its website.[3] It was reported that 143 officers took their own lives in 2016, 168 officers in 2017, 172 officers in 2018, and 228 officers in 2019.[4] *USA Today* and Blue H.E.L.P. also reported that 132 officers in 2019 were killed in the line of duty—a figure including deaths due to 9/11-related illnesses and heart attacks.[5] I'm confident that there are many more first responder deaths, either those we don't know of or ones not reported. The number of deaths is staggering. Some are natural deaths, and a few line-of-duty deaths we cannot control. But there are some we can. Right now, people need some hope to grasp hold of; let's give them that at all costs. In this book, there will be some people sharing their perspectives. These people are actual retired first responders, their spouses, my wife and children, and the message that you already received from Melissa in the Foreword section of this book. It's time for all to know what these law enforcement officers, medical personnel, and first responders and their families actually do, both on and off duty. No more sugar-coating these professions.

Lots of people have never experienced what the life of a police officer or first responder entails. I believe it is time to get

---

[3] Joel Shannon, "At Least 228 Police Officers Died by Suicide in 2019, Blue H.E.L.P. Says. That's More than Were Killed in the Line of Duty," *USA Today*, January 2, 2020, https://www.usatoday.com/story/news/nation/2020/01/02/blue-help-228-police-suicides-2019-highest-total/2799876001/.

[4] Ibid.

[5] Ibid.

it out in the open. People need to know; and when they find out, we must hope for a major pendulum swing to a more positive public perception. Don't get me wrong. I'm not an idiot, and I do know what goes on out there. Unfortunately, there are a few bad apples in the first responder profession, as is the case in all occupations. I know this because I had to personally arrest one or two of them during my service. Those few bad apples sadly affect the entire bushel and deserve the punishment required by their department and the criminal state statute. The one thing outstanding police officers cannot stand is bad police officers; it hurts us all. All law enforcement communities can go from hero to zero instantly, based on one bad cop. However, that does not deflect my belief that the good and righteous police officers and first responders deserve gratitude, kindness, and respect.

Let's get started.

CHAPTER 2

The Start of it All

I F YOU KNOW me personally, you know that I prefer to keep my life as private as possible. I'm sure most of you feel the same way. However, writing this book is bigger than that limitation. There is so much I've experienced; it would be an injustice not to put it on paper in order to help those traveling on the same road that I have.

Firstly, I want to give you some information about my background and where I came from prior to my being sworn-in as a police officer. We all have a journey that led us to the profession. I would love to hear yours someday. The Bible says, "I have much to write to you, but I do not want to use paper and ink. Instead, I hope to visit you and talk with you face-to-face, so that our joy may be complete."[6]

I was born on June 6, 1966. I was raised in a loving home with my mom, dad, and two older sisters whom I love unconditionally and consider my besties. Life growing up was fun and safe. We weren't wealthy, but we weren't broke either. My parents provided for us and met all our needs. I was never privy to any financial or

---

[6]   2 Jn 1:12 NIV

personal problems that they might've been having. I remember that we ate dinner every night at the table as a family, which is unfortunately one of the things missing in family life today. I enjoyed it when we sat down at the dinner table, and nobody was holding any electronic devices. The dinner table was used for prayer, to give thanks, and to discuss everybody's day. It was time to get to know one another and give support if needed. After we finished dinner, we would have a blast because it was straight from the dinner table to going outside, where I was always greeted by my best friends and all the other neighborhood crew. The block I grew up on was filled with a lot of wonderful people.

Another fond memory is of my high school years. The friends, relationships, teachers, and life lessons I learned back then were invaluable, and a lot of life-long friendships and memories were created there. I will never forget those days and the people that helped shape my future. I feel truly blessed to have had so many great people in my life during that time.

My parents were always incredibly supportive throughout my high school years and attended almost all my sporting events.

My parents became entrepreneurs at an early age and eventually fired their bosses. I inherited that trait more than you know at this point. I will always have a high level of respect for my parents because they always did what they said they would do.

My dad was somewhat strict with me, and prior to my high school graduation he gave me two options: option one was to enter the military; option two was to accept a one-way ticket to Alaska and work as a construction worker to help build a hunting lodge he was due to visit in August 1985. Both options were tough choices at the time because I had just started dating my future wife during our senior year of high school, and our relationship was only just beginning to really develop.

Since I had two choices, I chose the Alaska job. Two days after graduating from high school, I took off to Alaska. I'm pretty sure that was my Dad's way of helping me move into manhood. I returned several months later after completing the lodge, and life was good. My future wife and I picked up right where we had left off.

Unfortunately, life changed on August 18, 1985. After getting home from a date, I pulled up to my house and noticed several cars parked around the house, which was odd on account of it being so late. So, after seeing all the cars, I began to panic because I was certain something bad had happened to my dad. He was away on that 1985 Alaska hunting expedition. I was right on that one. As I walked into the house, my mom met me at the door. My oldest sister was sitting on the couch and crying uncontrollably. Mom was crying, but calm. Mom told me that my Dad's airplane had crashed in Alaska and he, along with everybody else on the plane, had been killed. The passengers on the plane were my dad, my brother-in-law Patrick (who was married to my older sister), Patrick's coworker and friend, and the Alaskan pilot. There were no survivors. My dad was forty-two years old when he died. Unfortunately, I don't remember who else was in the house that night. I just remember it being a blur.

What I do remember, however, is that after mom gave me the news, I ran outside, laid down on the hood of my Dad's Ford Bronco, and just screamed and cried in disbelief. Can you relate?

My brother-in-law Patrick and his friend, who were killed in the crash, were both active Denver firefighters whose futures were extremely bright at the time of their untimely deaths. The funeral was magnificent. The Denver Fire Department was brilliant, and the support of multiple other fire and police agencies and communities was also impressive. One of the largest churches in Denver was packed, and people lined the streets to show their support. Absolutely amazing!

I was nineteen when I received the news about my Dad's death. I was, and always will be, disappointed that my dad and I never really had the chance to get to know one another as I became an adult. But I am grateful for all the skills he taught me in the short amount of time we shared together. Love 'em if you got 'em; that's all I have to say about that.

Why do I share this story? It leads into the upcoming experiences throughout my police career when I saw many more deaths and much sadness. The loss of my dad was my first real death experience, and I remember how sad and lost I felt when it happened. My dad was the center of our family's foundation.

I carried that feeling with me my entire career when dealing with folks who had lost a loved one. I believe the experience made me a better police officer.

I share my dad's story because I genuinely believe that some people know when they're going to die. My dad did. I believe some first responders may harbor this fear as well...I know I did. So, if they know that they may die any day, why don't they make a change? Some police officers and other first responders know that there is a chance that they can die as soon as they pin on the badge, or put on their scrubs; but that doesn't stop them. Why? It's because every person who signs up to become a first responder has a true calling to help others. Cliché or not, that's a fact. They have a notion that they can make a difference; and let me tell you, they do. They feel a responsibility to help those unable to help themselves, to give people hope, and save lives.

The people in our country and within our communities are all our neighbors. That's why they do it. I also believe that police officers and first responders exist to help build God's kingdom, positively impact our community, and help change the world for the better.

The Bible says, "Love the Lord your God with all your heart and with all your soul and with all your strength and with all your mind and love your neighbor as yourself."[7]

So, here's the explanation of my aforementioned belief that my dad knew he was going to die. Dad was an avid hunter and fisherman, who had been on several hunting expeditions before his second trip to Alaska in 1985. That trip had first been planned

---

[7]   Lk 10:27 NIV

for 1978. But just prior to that, Dad was involved in an accident: an accident that unfortunately also involved me.

I was eleven at the time, and proud of the fact that I had just received my hunter safety card, and that I had completed the course on my own. My dad invited my older sister's husband, Patrick, and me to go on a hunting trip with him. I was never really a hunter, but it was a way to spend time with my dad.

On this hunting trip, we were out in the middle of nowhere in eastern Colorado, standing outside and simply enjoying the day. All of a sudden, my dad spotted a coyote. He yelled at us to get loaded up in the truck. My weapon was still loaded; it was a .22 long rifle. I told Dad that I had to unload my rifle before getting into his Bronco. Dad instructed me to unload it after I got in because the coyote was getting away. I knew from my hunter's safety class that getting into a vehicle with a loaded weapon was a big no-no.

After getting into the Bronco, Dad was now hellbent on catching that coyote. If you have never driven across an open field at approximately eighty miles an hour, you're missing out. I was bouncing all over the place while attempting to unload my rifle from the back seat.

I take full responsibility for what happened next: my rifle went off accidentally. To this day, I'm not sure exactly how the hell that happened. The bullet struck Dad on the outside of his right thigh, then exited behind his right knee. There was a lot of screaming from both Dad and me. But Patrick, the firefighter, remained calm.

Thankfully, Patrick was able to get from the front passenger seat and gain control of the vehicle. Patrick's cool disposition didn't surprise me because I knew he was a firefighter, which meant he had cultivated the innate ability to stay calm in the face of chaos.

It seemed as though a lifetime passed as we drove to a hospital approximately forty-five minutes away from where the accident occurred.

Once at the hospital, Dad advised the state trooper that he shot himself while stepping through a barbed-wire fence, which is what I was supposed to report as well. That didn't work out so well, because I always remember my parents telling me to never lie to the police. So, at eleven years of age, I took full responsibility for my actions and was prepared for my punishment. I'll tell you what: I was scared to death and thought I was going to prison for the remainder of my life.

However, there is a funny side to that story which involves the time I finally got to see my dad after his surgery. He stated, "You know son? I've been hunting my whole life, but you just started, and you've already shot something that I haven't." I laugh about that now, but I can tell you it was not funny at the time.

So, with that said, Dad's 1978 Alaska trip was canceled.

I tell that story because that was my first actual run-in with a law enforcement officer. I can still remember that state trooper's face as if it were yesterday; and I remember thinking how nice he was. I recall how professionally he handled the incident, and even the way he stood there keeping an upright posture. I remember his uniform being in perfect condition and the way he came across as an authority figure.

As scared as I was that day, I remember thinking to myself that when I grew up, I wanted to be just like that state trooper someday. Just FYI, I did not do any prison time!

I also earned a great deal of respect for firearms that day, what they are capable of, and how quickly an accident can change lives. I can proudly tell you there was never an accidental discharge of any firearm or safety issue on my part after that day. So, that was the segue leading up to my explanation of why I think some people (my dad and myself included) know when they're going to die.

My dad somewhat recovered from the shooting accident in 1977, and he went on that re-scheduled 1985 Alaska trip. I'm pretty sure he knew that he shouldn't go because he was having some health issues at the time. He still had only limited use of his right leg, so walking was a challenge. In addition to that, my mom later told me that approximately a week before Dad left, he took out his first-ever life insurance policy. Also, a week after he arrived in Alaska, he called us and told us all that he loved us, which he never did on any of his other hunting trips. He also said that he was thinking of giving up his rifle for a camera because he had really been enjoying taking pictures of the wild animals more than harvesting them. It was just a few days after receiving that call we found out that his plane crashed, and that all on board had been killed. Devastating! I'm sure some of you can relate to that.

My dad did, however, get to see and stay at the lodge that he had me build after my high school graduation in 1984. I believe that the accident in 1977 was God's way of keeping my dad with us a bit longer. But since he had a passion for hunting, he was compelled to keep doing it.

I believe that the feeling is true with law enforcement and first responders as well. They have so much love, passion, and dedication for what they do. It's why they continue doing it, with full knowledge that they could be killed on any given day.

Other than Dad knowing his death was near. He always told us that in the event of his death, we were to spread his ashes over the Alaskan range. Ironic how that played out!

So, in summary, this chapter relates to law enforcement because it deals with my first experience with firearm capabilities, police officer roles (the state trooper), and the death and sadness surrounding the loss of a loved one.

What's so unbelievable is this: even though first responders know that they could die in their line of work, they continue to take risks for all of us!

So, the journey of life continues!

CHAPTER 3

The Life Journey

AFTER DAD DIED, it was a matter of picking up the pieces and moving forward. One thing my dad taught us was to never quit and never to give up on our dreams.

There was a rough patch we all went through, which caused me, my mom, and my sisters to become a bit distant from one another. But that did not last long. We all pulled together and got past that issue. My eldest sister struggled the longest, which was expected. It's not every day you lose your dad and your husband on the same day. We have discovered over the years that she is an extremely strong person. We all have had our own internal battles to fight through.

Moving forward on June 28, 1986, the hottest day of that year (101 degrees), now at the age of twenty, I married my high school sweetheart and my soul mate. My wife and I worked various jobs to support our luxury two-bedroom apartment. We shared the apartment with several cockroaches and silverfish. My wife and I used to joke about it, treating the cockroaches like pets—we even named some of them at one point!

I was twenty-two when we had our first baby: a little girl.

Through all the jobs that I held, and from my wife's income, we were able to buy our first house. I think our house payment was around $600 a month, and we were scared to death because we weren't sure how we were going to make that payment. We drove junk cars but survived.

Approximately four years later, we had our second baby: a little boy. My wife and I had some ups and downs but never gave up on each another. We married young and had a lot of learning to do.

After our boy was born, we were able to buy a bigger house—one with a little bit of property. We enjoyed life, and loved camping, fishing, and spending time with our family and friends.

Unfortunately, in 1995, my father-in-law died. He was a great man and would give you the shirt off his back without being asked. He never gave up on supporting his family, especially after he hit some tough times. He did what it took to survive. Again, devastating!

Life continues, right? I still could not shake the feeling that I had a greater purpose in life. I wanted to do something meaningful.

I took an entry-level job working in the corporate world. I knew it was not my chosen profession, but that's the way it happened. I am, however, proud that I worked my way up from the bottom to a high-level position. I even had some healthy stock options, which I later cashed out and spent frivolously.

I managed to put myself into the police academy. I knew I was destined to help people and be in a position of importance. Being a cop was the answer and it was something I always wanted to do since the age of eleven and all throughout high school.

So, I went for it.

CHAPTER 4

The Hiring Journey

A T AGE THIRTY, I enrolled in the Community College of Aurora, Lowry Campus Police Academy, to obtain my POST-certification. My time at the police academy lasted for eleven months, totaling 637 hours of scenario-based training, bookwork, firearms training, driving training, video training, physical fitness, arrest control, etc. Speaking of arrest control: a special thanks to my wife and kids, who were arrested and placed into handcuffs several hundred times throughout my time at the academy. Sorry about all the missing skin!

Some people never made it out of the academy solely due to the sometimes-graphic nature of the training. Some people never pursued the profession, even after graduating.

On November 19, 1997, graduation took place; and I received my POST certificate from the Law Enforcement Training Academy Peace Officer Standards and Training Board.

The certificate read as follows:

November 19, 1997 B—4135

For having satisfactorily passed the Standardized Examination as prescribed for certification for appointment as a Colorado peace officer. This certificate expires three years from the date of issuance unless the certificate holder meets the requirements for continued certification as established by state law and the P.O.S.T. Board.

This certificate was signed by the governor of the state of Colorado, who was Roy Romer at the time, and the Attorney General, State of Colorado P.O.S.T. Board Chairperson. I just thought that was so cool.

Side note here: I think I surprised a bunch of my family members and friends because they were not one hundred percent certain that I was cut out for that line of work. There wasn't anyone in our family tree, that I know of, who had held a badge.

Once I was out of the academy, I knew the agency I wanted to work for, and took a position as a reserve police officer offered there. I was excited about receiving that position because it allowed me to get my foot in the door and at the time, several people were wanting to get into law enforcement. Law enforcement jobs were a bit scarce back in the day. Now, in 2020, that's not the problem. There are not enough people wanting to apply, probably due to the negative stigma the news loves to share and the high number of officer deaths.

I hope, somehow, the information in this book can improve the knowledge of the haters and increase the respect that law enforcement deserves so that more people will apply for duty. Police officers, I believe, are the shepherds protecting the sheep from the wolves.

In addition to conducting my duties as a reserve police officer, I was asked if I wanted to accept a full-time, paid position as a department dispatcher while waiting for a position to open up in patrol. Since I did not have a paying job at the time, I graciously accepted the dispatcher position. People talk about a difficult job—I had no idea what the role involved. Not only did you have to deal with unruly people on the telephone, but the patrol officers had attitudes of their own when they came over the radio. I was grateful for that position because it taught me so much about what our dispatchers go through.

Working as a dispatcher (also known as 911 Operators) is where the actual saving of life begins. Have you ever picked up a telephone, and the only thing you hear is high-pitched, blood-curdling screaming and you're unable to make out the words? How do you stay calm? How do you know what's happening on the other end of the line, or where is it happening? How do you get the information needed to get first responders on their way? Good question, but that's what dispatchers do; you should ask them about it someday.

If you ever get the opportunity to sit inside a dispatch center, particularly on a Saturday evening, I recommend you take it up; it's a real eye-opener.

I have the highest level of respect for the dispatchers. If you ever meet one, thank them. So, not long after starting my role as a dispatcher, our department opened up the hiring process for one police officer. Unfortunately, I did not get that position but continued with my reserve police officer duties and my dispatcher role.

It wasn't long after that two additional spots opened up in patrol, and I was offered one of them. That was one of the top five best days of my life. Man, talk about proud! After all, this was a position that everybody wanted at that time. The pay was okay and the benefits were good. But I did notice, however, that the retirement benefits were not that great—it was a 401(k), not a pension, as I had expected. After all, I was willing to put my life on the line. But I didn't care; I was a cop.

A side note, I've heard the retirement program has improved over the years.

I had no idea how that would affect the rest of my life; I didn't really care nor think about it at the time, which is another thing that has inspired me to write this book.

So, after accepting the position, the next step was to get sworn in—the day I had been looking forward to for a long time. My swearing-in date was November 9, 1998. I never doubted I was going to get the position because I pretty much felt like it was my calling. But wow, it was really happening now. So it was a proud day! Off I went to the swearing-in ceremony at the town hall. It was me and one other guy, who is still involved in law enforcement and my life today. I love him and his family a lot. The swearing-in process was a little cheesy. There was no big celebration. No swearing-in in front of a crowd, nope! My partner and I were sworn in by one lady inside a broom closet. I'm not kidding! I guess there were no conference rooms available at the time. But whatever, I was a cop, and it was still one of my best days ever.

I held up my right hand and I repeated the following:

I, Steven J. Eastin, do solemnly swear by the ever-living God, that I will support the Constitution of the United States and the state of Colorado, and faithfully perform the duties of the office of a police officer upon which I am about to enter.

I then got to sign Form 827, the Oath of Office.

I knew then that my job was to enforce the laws handed down by the state, which I knew I would do with honor, integrity, and respect for all the people whom I was about to serve and protect.

A side-note: I know the swearing-in process has improved a lot, and the departments have stepped up their game in that area. It's now a well-deserved celebration for the new officer and their families. Well done!

Next was the fun part: getting my badge (# 98-05/the fifth hire in 1998), uniforms, a gun, toys on my gun-belt (which I had no idea how to use), a bulletproof vest, my own name tag, shiny boots. All very cool, right? It really was a highlight. I never thought I would be adding another thirty pounds to my wardrobe.

I felt like Superman when I put on that uniform. Then, wow! I got my own locker. I later named the locker as my memory closet because I stored lots of memories in there throughout the years, such as family photos, gifts, and notes from my wife and children. I kept adding memories to my locker because I knew if I were to die in the line of duty, my family could look through it. They would see how important they really were to me and how much I loved them, even though I didn't always demonstrate it.

Next, the FTO program: It was made known at the time that I would probably get washed out, meaning canned, before completing. You'd better have a backbone and be able to take a whole bunch of shit from your FTO, as well as from the people on the street. That improved somewhat before I left. We tried keeping everyone, and I know this because I served as a field training officer for approximately half of my career. Today, I think that was just a scare tactic to toughen us up. The FTO program was a great test to demonstrate how much patience you really had. The training program consisted of multiple tests, multiple live scenarios, firearm training, arrest control, physical fitness, driving tactics, tools training, radar certification, Taser certification, and mapping to learn a city I really knew nothing about.

I found out much about myself during the training, including my level of courage. My mind was full of questions: Am I going to make it? Can I learn everything? Do I feel fear? Am I aggressive enough? Can I learn the right mindset? Can I learn the Colorado Revised Statutes? Can I endure pain? Can I win in a fight? Can I handle adrenaline, tension, and anxiety? Am I tolerant? Can I handle torment, control my emotions, and keep my temper? Do I have sympathy or empathy? Am I happy, mad, or sad? Can I learn the booking and jail process? Will I stay alive, or will I get hurt? Who are my friends, and who can I trust? Not to mention, can I be an unlicensed counselor, social worker, doctor, or therapist on the fly? Holy smokes! Talk about a roller coaster ride of emotions and a learning curve, right? Can you relate? How many of you know what I'm talking about? How many of you want this job?

But, after all that, I earned the right to graduate the FTO program, and officially became a solo police officer.

So, let's go patrolling!

CHAPTER 5

The Patrol Journey: On Duty

B ECOMING A SOLO cop was the greatest feeling. I was assigned my own patrol car. Cool, right? No more FTO telling me what to do all the time. I could do whatever I wanted now, right up until the point that the dispatcher sent me to my first solo call for service over the radio. When the call comes out, what goes through your mind is, "Now what? What's my call sign, what was the address they just said, what kind of call is it? Shit, where is my map book?" Remember, there was no GPS at that time, folks. My brain scrambled, "Do I do a normal response, code two lights, code three lights and siren?" "Where should I park, who's going with me, what am I investigating, what type of crime is it?" The list goes on and on. But whatever you do, don't sound stupid over the radio because you'll never live it down, and you don't want the proverbial write up. I think there was a sergeant or two who enjoyed that just a little too much.

So, after all that, you finally arrive on the scene. Then, you're wondering what code do I choose—there's one through ten, so you take your pick, and pray that you don't have to call Code Adam. I'll talk more about that later. Oh, and that code ten thing, keep that one in mind too. We'll talk more about that later in the chapter on retirement. Now that you're finally on scene, you start making contacts and do whatever it takes to bring the situation to a peaceful resolution. But you also must make sure you get back to the PD and finish your paperwork before the end of your shift because there's no approved overtime. After a year or so, the job started going a lot more smoothly.

I think that we can all agree that becoming a cop involves a pretty big learning curve. In all seriousness, I thank all you FTO's for your patience, hard work, and dedication. You truly set the tone for how rookie police officers and first responders conduct themselves for the remainder of their careers.

During my career, I spent many years on patrol responding to calls for service. I was first promoted to field training officer, and then to patrol supervisor (where I served as a corporal). I also had the privilege of being an instructor in different training topics. In 2006, I was the first sworn police officer from our agency to attend the crisis intervention team (CIT) program. My department's CIT mission statement at that time was: "The Mission of the Crisis Intervention Program is to use understanding in skills gained through specific training to identify and provide the most effective and compassionate response possible to police situations involving people in a mental health crisis."[8]

I had the honor of supervising that program for several years. CIT officers were typically requested to respond to most of the calls that involved servicing citizens experiencing mental health

---

[8]   "CIT & CIP Training," NAMI Greater Milwaukee, accessed July 29, 2020, https://www.namigrm.org/cit-cip-training.

issues. That position was very demanding and required a high degree of attention on a daily basis, even on my off days. Many of my CIT citizens had my cell number. There were times I would get calls from them at two or three in the morning when they were in distress. Even though I was typically able to calm them down, I would have an on-duty CIT officer respond to their home. I never really got used to being woken up out of a dead sleep by someone screaming at me on the phone that they were about to take their own life or that of another. But I can say this: I really did care.

Now, to my most prized position: the Emergency Response Team (ERT) Police Negotiator. This position was very rewarding. But there was also another huge learning curve because an officer can never get enough training on that subject. There was also a lot of on-the-job training that came with it. The accomplishments that my team and I completed were amazing, and most of the calls for service that came in while I held that position typically ended with a peaceful resolution. While serving as the police negotiator, my agency awarded me negotiator of the year.

I really did love my job! Just so you know, it was the last couple of years where I found myself entering different stages of the career. For example, I could not shut things off anymore. I started becoming reclusive and saddened by what I saw. What I'm saying here is that you need to pay attention to the negative stages and, if need be, get out of the profession. Don't wait until it's too late.

WARNING—So, here's the point where things become X-rated.

I'm going to start this section with a line from one of my favorite movies, *Courageous*. If you have not seen that movie yet, I highly recommend it. As the main actor is speaking to a group of people at a church, he says: "Being a cop forced me to see the worst in people and to see how one person's selfish decision can hurt so many others." When I heard that line, it felt as if things came full circle for me. I began to tear-up, and I had no idea why other than that it summed up how I felt.

Let's investigate some of the types of calls for service my partners and I got to handle over the next eighteen years on patrol. The calls for service ranged across all kinds of situations: theft, fights in progress, domestic violence, child abuse, bar fights, civil assists, citizen assists, car break-ins, damaged property, shots fired, disturbances and suicide calls, natural deaths, drunk or drug calls, DUI calls, traffic accidents, traffic pursuits (where you must have the phonetic alphabet from A-Z down pat), missing persons and runaways—the list goes on and on. And, oh yeah, don't forget to write your citations and complete your field interview cards to keep those stats up—it was very important to keep those stats up to date (a requirement from the upper management).

WARNING, the following is not for the sensitive, so skip the rest of this chapter if you have a weak stomach or bad dreams. This is where you learn about what first responders really do, see, hear, smell, taste, and feel.

My first arrest call was also my first resisting arrest call. Remember, prior to this cop job, I worked in customer service in an office and my last fight was in high school. This call was my first real knock-down and drag-out physical altercation. These are the types of calls that separate the men from the boys, and the women from the girls. If you survived or won the fight, you might start earning some respect amongst your peers. If you lost, you might be deemed as weak and require additional training. The suspect I faced that day was a lot larger than me, and I later found out he was a career felon. I still thank him to this day because if he'd wanted to, he could've won that night, and I'm pretty sure looking back on it now that he knew it.

One thing about career felons is that they typically don't have anything to lose, and they don't care about you or who is at home waiting for you to return, usually because all they care about is not going back to jail. Really!

Here are a few detailed examples of calls for service that a police officer can face during a typical shift:

Calls for service regarding mental health subjects: Remember that CIT responsibility that I spoke of earlier? Those types of calls for service came in daily and required tons of paperwork, but I enjoyed them because these folks were getting the referrals that they truly needed. It was overwhelming at times. I just wish we had had more to offer at the time. Mental health people could be any gender or age. For a time, I was one of the only CIT trained officers in my department, which allowed me to become immersed in the field, and it quickly became a passion of mine.

One particular call concerned a juvenile woman who chose to cut deep lacerations on her arms and legs. She said that it made her feel better and released stress. Hmm, right? While I was on the scene, she kept talking to, and seemed in fear of, a "large, scary man" who wanted to harm her—but whom no one else could see. Nevertheless, the young woman was physically shaking. Although I couldn't see the man (because he did not exist), and being the good officer I was, I told the young woman that I wouldn't let the man harm her. Next stop, we took her to the hospital, where she would be placed on a seventy-two hour mental health evaluation. It was later determined that she was completely sober. So, I completed the mental health holding documentation, gave referrals, and then went on to the next call for service.

Next, I had another call for service regarding an adult natural death. A male collapsed in his garage. CPR terminated Code Adam (told you we would talk about that Code Adam again). The man died right there in front of me. I remember investigating the scene and taking pictures of the deceased when I suddenly thought the body moved, and the guy's eyes had opened. My sergeant said that was normal. Huh? It sure didn't seem normal. I just couldn't grasp that he was dead and that he had died right in front of my eyes. That damned CPR always works in the movies, right?

There were many calls for service regarding suicide. I can't remember exactly how many. There were just too damned many of them, especially around the holiday season. It came in all

78

varieties. Had the person hanged themselves from a closet or jumped in front of a moving train? Had they pulled into their garage, shut the door, rolled up the windows, and started the engine? Were they male, female, adult, or a juvenile? Had a firearm been involved, or maybe a drug overdose? Were there witnesses, or had the person made sure to take their life in private? So many possibilities! But nobody had ever told me in the police academy or the FTO program that cops were part of the cleanup crew. I can't tell you how many times we cleaned up blood, brains, and other internal organs with rags and a bucket. I specifically did this so the family members would not have to see the aftermath. Let's just leave it at that.

Side note: When someone pulls their car into the garage, seals it shut, and starts their car engine up, they die by carbon monoxide poisoning. The first time I experienced such a call, I learned to be careful when moving the deceased body. This is why: the deceased's skin has basically been melted from the bones, and peels off in your hands just by touching it. A rookie officer and I learned this the hard way—let's just call it on-the-job training.

Most upsetting are the calls for service regarding an infant death. One I attended had been staged as an accident by a male subject, not the father, a boyfriend. Staged to be an accident? No! Doctors are smart, and bruises and broken bones are easy to detect. And why had the boyfriend done this? All because the baby would not stop crying. Are you kidding me? I'm sorry, I just don't understand this one at all.

Things to know about dead bodies: There is typically a very specific odor that accompanies the death process. Prior to moving the body, don't forget that a large amount of air can sometimes come out of the deceased-mouth. So, fair warning, stay away from that area. Also, watch out for the loss of control of their bowels. Learned this one the hard way, too! A tip: Keep Vicks Vapor Rub on hand at all times to put in your nose prior to entering a death scene. The worst thing about the odor is that you can smell it for several days afterwards and even after several showers.

Another piece of the puzzle of someone's death is that someone has to do a notification, which means telling the spouse, parent, etc. And who gets to do that? A police officer and a victim's advocate!

One notification I was involved in concerned telling the parents that their teenage child had died in a car accident. We went to the parent's home and gave the mother and father the news. The father ran through the house, screaming the child's name, hoping that we were wrong. The mother collapsed at the front door. Once the father realized that it was true, he collapsed on the floor next to his wife, and cried and yelled in anger for several minutes before composing himself enough to talk with us. Very sad!

If you don't know what a victim's advocate does, then find out. These people are amazing and often go unrecognized. I had the privilege of working with the same victim's advocate at my agency for my entire career. The lives that lady changed for the better and those she saved are countless, not to mention, she kept my sanity in check. I will always be grateful for her and cherish her friendship.

Just a little secret I'll share: I had the privilege of praying to myself over every dead body I was ever involved with; #thankful.

Had enough? Nope, four hours left in the shift, so let's keep going.

Then there are the calls for service regarding a sexual assault. Disgusting! Woman beaten, body scarred, and mutilated, and for what! It still beats me how a human being can inflict this on another helpless person.

I remember one call for service regarding child abuse, which involved the biological father sexually torturing his four-year-old daughter with various objects during his parenting weekend appointed to him by the courts. What can you say? Calls for service regarding domestic violence were common. One concerned a pissed-off, jealous spouse who decided "if not mine, then nobody's." It involved an all-night session of mental and physical torture for the woman. It's tough to even try to imagine it! You can't make this shit up.

Had enough? Nope, we're still on duty, so let's take a few more calls for service before heading into the PD to cram all the necessary paperwork into an hour.

Calls for service for SWAT and negotiation team call-outs typically become very long nights with no sleep.

Now, let's talk about the calls for service that will stick with you for a long time or maybe even a lifetime. No. Really? That can happen? Sure, it can.

One call for service I'll never forget was when a parent decided to attempt to take their own life, which failed. However, before attempting this, the parent first chose to kill their juvenile children. This particular call is etched in my memory and here's why. It was the one time I recalled that almost every responder broke down and cried publicly. I also vividly remember the suspect's eyes. The only way I can describe them is that they were empty and held no soul. I'm not sure if you can understand that, but that's what I felt that day.

Another call for service came when a parent chose to kill all their children, drive to the police department with them, then shoot up the building with one intention, to kill officers, and to be killed by them. We call that one *Suicide by Cop*.

I will tell you that all the murders in these scenarios were over something trivial or stupid, like custody issues. Really, are you kidding me? Sadly, no. There is no simple answer to that question. How do you comprehend something like that? Why is it that two grown adults cannot figure out how to peacefully raise and share their children? Why and how do innocent children become the victims of this? Figure it out, people!

"You have heard that it was said to the people long ago, 'You shall not murder, and anyone who murders will be subject to judgment.'"[9]

This next call was an eye-opener: It involved investigating an incident involving a vicious dog. I never expected the dog owner

---

[9]   Mt 5:21 NIV

to hold a shotgun to my face. I never saw that one coming, but it all worked out just fine—he ended up with just a slap on the wrist. I know for sure that he got out of that one with nothing more than a citation.

Then there was one call for service that hits close to home for many of us all over the world . . . unfortunately on a daily basis. It's a Code Ten, meaning "Officer In Trouble." But you must be patient, as we will talk more about Code Ten in chapter nine.

Police officers are regularly shot at by suspects for no real reason, and without any conscience or remorse apparent from the shooter. Now, step that up to a zillion, to all the "Officer Down" scenarios, where police officers are daily ambushed and murdered while eating their already rushed meal, or while sitting in their patrol cars completing reports, or while on-scene conducting business to win a peaceful resolution.

I have only been involved in one funeral procession for a highly respected police officer who was killed in the line of duty. That was one of the worst days of my life, and so many other lives were affected as well. The impact on the lives of so many people who were affected by that officer's death was overwhelming.

I'll repeat, these suspects have no real reason for doing what they do, have no conscience or remorse, and have zero concern for the first responder's spouse or children waiting for them at home.

And, please, don't forget about the first responders' mom and dad, brothers and sisters, aunts and uncles, nieces and nephews, cousins, in-laws, friends, and acquaintances.

Why? Why do these suspects do it? STOP IT! No acceptable answer exists in the world for that question. Please take these police officers and first responders' lives and family members' lives into consideration before you do something stupid. I promise you that if you don't, you will regret it! I'm begging you! Don't do it! Why would you want to spend your life in prison or be put to death? Think about it!

I also want to mention a few more things, like the alert tone that comes over the radio to notify officers that an urgent "In progress" call is coming. That in itself will make your butt pucker up. We'll talk more about the alert tone in chapter nine.

Then, consider the first responders who work the night shift and who, when they do get home to get some sleep, close their eyes only to face the red and blue flashing lights that they've been looking at for most of the night.

Or how about the fear of contracting diseases? I can't count how many times drunk or pissed-off combatants spit on me or in my face, or get their vomit on me. And don't forget about the urine and feces that was always such fun to clean up. Try getting that out of the patrol car! Shout out to the firefighters for helping out in that area as well.

Why is it that drunk people have such a hard time controlling their bladder and bowel movements? Pretty sure you all know the answer to that one.

So, now that we're done talking about the rich variety of calls for service, how do you cope with all that on a daily basis? Well, I did what most first responders still do—joked about it with other peers. Our excuse was that it was our way of releasing all the stress. I can tell you what I did frequently: Go to my favorite, secluded, desolate areas around town; and de-escalate by parking my patrol car for a few minutes, just sitting there to pray, and then cry. That's how I coped with it at the time. During the last couple of years of my career, I'd also vent to my wife. I'm pretty sure that wasn't neither healthy nor fun for her.

During my tour of duty, there was not a whole lot of external or internal peer support/resources available. Nor did I feel that it was safe to go down the path of having a mental breakdown. It was just the mindset you had to maintain: Cops are always in control, and cannot show any weakness. Not to do so could be career suicide, or "Termination," as it's officially known. You never shared your true feelings. I did, however, know that there was a dedicated off site counselor who we could privately call if needed, although this information was not highly publicized.

Knowing my old agency and its chief, I feel certain that they have progressed in that area. So I reached out to them when I was writing this book. I phoned my old chief and discussed my purpose in writing the book. I asked him about what arrangements they now have for providing peer support to cops and employees. I wasn't surprised to find they now have a peer support group program in place, which is run by one of my old sergeants from back in the day, who is now a commander. I received permission from my chief to speak to him, and you will see what he had to say in another chapter of this book.

On a lighter note, we were never taught in the academy that drunk people are often found naked, though I'm not sure why that is. But I can tell you that I saw more nakedness in my career than I could ever imagined or care about! Typically, not a pretty sight. However, there was one particular noise complaint call for service I vividly recall. It happened during a snowstorm and involved four naked ladies, a lot of wine, and a hot tub. The ladies refused to get dressed and turned down my offer of a towel each. Trust me, I had plenty of backup on this call. The ladies were given a warning for the noise complaint and were asked to move their party inside, which they did.

Don't get me wrong; not all the calls for service were awful. Somewhere I came away with a sense of satisfaction and joy. That's the reason why first responders do what they do. For instance, you might get the opportunity to save a life, or a marriage, or say something positive that might stick with someone for life (or at least long enough that they may make a change for the better). Sometimes, it's just about having the opportunity to give somebody who is down on their luck a compliment, a cup of coffee, or food or clothing, or a room for the night, and possibly some hope for the future. Unfortunately, these types of positive calls for service cannot erase the memories of the bad ones . . . at least, not for me.

Although it was frowned upon back then, I still took advantage of praying with, and for, people on a daily basis. I will repeat this Bible quote: "Love the Lord your God with all your heart and with all your soul and with all your strength and with all your mind; and, Love your neighbor as yourself"[10]

Now, take all the calls for service above and throw in about a hundred other different types of calls for service. While you're at it, multiply those that I've mentioned by another hundred, and you're getting a clearer picture of the sheer volume of calls. Of course, some of the scenarios were the same, but the locations, names, and faces were different.

I often wonder how many arrests, dead bodies, and death notifications I actually made, and how many calls for service I responded to during those eighteen years of service. I often think about those first responders who serve for thirty years plus; how many hundreds of service calls have they responded to?

Why do I share these stories? Because I want people to know what police officers and first responders do, see, hear, smell, taste, and touch. I want it to be the most respected profession in the world. I want police officers and all first responder suicide rates to go down . . . or better yet, to be eradicated. I want the in-the-line-of-duty deaths and murders to stop! I want first responders to know that there are people out here rooting for you, and that there are resources available to support you. I want the families of the first responders to know that as well. First responders have to deal with things that are just not normal and are hard for the human brain to process. These things become permanently ingrained in our subconscious mind. How do you

10 Lk 10:27 NIV

deal with that? How do we get rid of the nightmares? Many first responders suffer from PTSD (Post Traumatic Stress Disorder), a mental disorder that develops after experiencing or witnessing a terrifying or life-threatening event. How do first responders deal with suicidal thoughts, and how do they stop thinking about all the things that their eyes have seen, or they've heard, or smelled over a long period of time? Good question! How do your loved ones deal with the effects of it upon you? Stand by!

Now, you have an idea about the types of situations that first responders have to deal with everyday, and how they can have an adverse emotional effect on a long-term basis.

Before moving on, I want to discuss who is actually involved in a police officer's call for service. Let's start from the top. It begins with a victim or suspect who generates a call for service. Something bad has to happen, right? Anyone could be making that call for service; it could be the victim, the suspect, a family member, a friend, or a neighbor. You won't know till you get there. When the call gets to our dispatcher, they might find themselves on the receiving end of somebody completely hysterical (to the point where they are unintelligible). I guarantee you that a dispatcher's blood pressure goes up just a little! However, they are trained to remain calm, gather as much information as possible, and get first responders en route to attend to the chaos. Would you want to be a dispatcher? The job is a multi-tasking nightmare. Dispatchers are the very first responders and know the scene only through the information they can collect over the phone. Do you think once a dispatcher retires that they forget about events from their career? Hopefully, they can, but I'm pretty sure the answer to that one is a "no." As I've said before, if you ever meet a dispatcher, hug them, and thank them for what they do. I would appreciate that, and I'm sure they will.

Next up, police and fire. At this point, the task is to get to the call and get things under control as fast as possible, so that you're available for the next one. Police officers often have to solve people's problems, which may have taken years to manifest. They must try to solve those problems in a very short period of time, typically less than 30 minutes or so. Next, they must contact the victim's advocate if needed, and get the detectives en route. The worst-case scenario at this stage is having to call the coroner because someone is dead (Code Adam). It just creeps me out that when we die, we end up in the back of the coroner's pickup truck. I never liked that aspect of the death calls.

It just amazes me how one person's wrong choice can involve so many civilians and first responders.

I also want to share with you some general expectations people have of police officers; and if you don't believe me, just search the internet or watch the news. Speaking of the news, my suggestion is to not believe everything you hear. There are a lot more facts that the public does not get to know. Seek the facts before you judge!

Back to the expectations: go to the internet and type in police.unc.edu, and this is what you will find.

Qualities of a Police Officer

Humanity: We respect life and liberty. We are sensitive and inclusive, treating everyone with dignity and compassion.

Integrity: We are guided by the principles of justice. We employ the highest ethical standard, we demand accountability, consistency, fairness, and honesty, and the performance of our duties.

Professionalism: We take pride in our department. We are committed to excellence in our profession, and we maintain the highest standard of education in our field.

Courage: Maintain a mental and moral strength to resist opposition and fairness of mind. Always stand by your fellow officers in the face of danger or extreme difficulty. Position duties are inclusive of all required tasks. Employees perform other related work as required.[11]

Duties of a Police Officer

- Protects life and property through the enforcement of laws and regulations
- Proactively patrols assigned areas
- Responds to calls for police service

---

[11] "Mission," Mission | Police - Miami University, accessed July 29, 2020, https://miamioh.edu/police/about/mission/index.html.

- Conducts preliminary and follow up criminal and traffic investigations
- Conducts interviews
- Prepares written reports and filled notes of investigations and patrol activities
- Arrests and processes criminals
- Testifies in court
- Emergency duties required during adverse weather conditions
- Ability to exercise judgment in determining when to use force and to what degree
- Operate law enforcement vehicles under emergency conditions, day or night
- Comprehending emergency personnel at accident emergencies and disasters
- Commanding emergency personnel at accident emergencies and disasters
- Takes an active role in community-oriented policing
- Self-initiate traffic and or criminal investigations[12]

Wow, that's a lot. That's why first responders train every waking hour. Could you complete all those different calls for service that I outlined earlier daily, several times repeatedly, while at the same time remembering all the expectations above,

---

[12] "Officer Expectations and Duties," The University of North Carolina at Chapel Hill, accessed July 29, 2020, https://police.unc.edu/recruitment/officer-expectations-duties/.

and still actually doing your job? Well, that's what police officers and first responders have to do.

Now, let me share a couple of fun facts. Soon after I was sworn-in, one of my higher-ranking officers deemed my nickname to be EZ E. That comes from an old Commodore's tune you may know, *Easy Like a Sunday Morning*. The name stuck with me my entire career, even after I was promoted to corporal when it switched to Cpl. E. I'm still very proud of that nickname and title.

A couple more side notes: I tried to come into work each day with a positive attitude. When I entered the locker room, I would typically break out into a song: usually *Easy Like a Sunday Morning* or the Alicia Keys hit *This Girl Is On Fire*.

If it was a Wednesday, we enjoyed making fun of the Camel commercial about "hump day," which seemed to go on forever, although some younger readers probably don't recognize that old commercial. If you really want to know, then ask one of your older friends or Google it!

Also, after we all got dressed to prepare for our daily briefing, I would stand in front of the mirror and tell the guys, "I don't know about all you guys, but damn I look good!" I did that for most of my career, and it never got old. At least, not for me!

Now, let's get personal!

CHAPTER 6

The Personal Journey: Off Duty

S o, LET'S TALK about the personal, off duty journey. What do
police officers and first responders, including me, do when
not actually on duty? I do recognize that the first responders are
typically never off duty in their minds, but let's focus on their
hobbies, and what they do at home with their families.

First, I want to talk about the reason why first responders are
never off duty. With all those calls for service that we discussed in
chapter five, especially if an arrest was made or a citation issued,
comes a whole lot of paperwork, which creates a whole lot of
court time. It was amazing to me how my court appearances
were typically scheduled on my days off, and somehow, never fit
the schedule. Nine times out of ten, court appearances disrupted
my sleeping schedule. In the law enforcement world, sleep will
always be a luxury. The office would call, then there would be a
SWAT call-out, and maybe court appearances, with limited time
to spend on family commitments, which would be squeezed in
to try to keep everyone happy.

It's not that easy when you're taking a vacation, either,
because you have to make several notifications to warn the
courts (municipal, state, and county) that you're taking a few days

off and won't be able to appear. If you're not in court, then it's highly likely that some type of training class is scheduled. Not to mention, when off duty, first responders are always trained to know and be aware of their surroundings. So, how the hell are first responders supposed to relax? Good question!

One of the reasons I called this chapter *The Personal Journey: Off Duty* is because I know that the majority of first responders I worked with, had a lot going on in their personal lives, and that included me. Some had financial issues, marital issues, alcohol issues, behavioral issues, anger issues, gambling issues, faith issues, PTSD issues—the list is endless. I will say it again, that included me.

In this chapter, I will share some of the challenges my family and I had to persevere and overcome. I have chosen to share this information not to expose my dirty laundry, faults, or weaknesses while serving, but because I believe in my heart that someone out there has similar challenges and experiences that need working through. If, by telling my own story, I touch one person or a million in a positive manner or help save a life or a relationship, then I will have accomplished one of the many goals for writing this book and sharing my story. I want all first responders to know that with the right mindset, courage, and a good support system, you can get through almost anything.

On that note, I should tell you that during my eighteen years of service, my support team was my wife, two children, many family members and friends, which was definitely an advantage for me. I also gained a son-in-law on January 3, 2009. God truly blessed our family with his addition, and I'm proud of him.

I didn't always consider my family and friends as my support team, because I was a police officer and didn't need one, right? Police and first responders typically must keep up the facade of having no weaknesses, being the strong one, and always being in control of all situations. But, in reality, we're all human.

Throughout my long years of police service, I held multiple other jobs. I had my own trucking company that hauled dirt, rock, and asphalt locally in my Colorado community and the Colorado mountains. I was the general contractor of my own construction company, which developed a community in eastern Colorado and constructed new homes from the ground up. I also bought cars that needed repair and flipped them for a few dollars over my cost to folks in need of transportation.

Side note: I pretty much always lost money on the car deals because I honestly enjoyed giving them away.

The final business I owned and operated was a trailer refurbishing company, which I ran from my own home.

Mind you, at one point during my police career, all these businesses were fully operational simultaneously.

I managed the employees, did the accounting, scheduling, spent time at all the locations, swung hammers, turned wrenches, painted cars, repaired tires; you name it, and I did it all, while at the same time performing my police duties to a high standard.

I hardly ever slept, but, damn, I had a goal to be a millionaire and a successful entrepreneur by the time I was forty-four. That's what I told my wife when I asked her to marry me.

This pursuit of becoming an entrepreneur millionaire went on for years. At one point, the money was rolling in, but, unbeknownst to me, my relationships were suffering because of my selfish goal. Should I also mention my number one addiction—gambling? I could spend $3000 a night, either in cash or credit cards, at the casinos and not bat an eye. That was one of the reasons why I got so excited when the department sent me to Las Vegas for a three-day officer survival course. Not good; that one cost me a bunch!

If I saw a way to make a buck, I took it; just ask my wife. Twice I came home and told her to start packing because I had sold our house. No kidding, I actually did that, although I'm not proud of it. Not recommended activity for husbands! But, back then, I was the type of guy who thought he needed no one's permission.

Why did I work so hard and have so many things going on? Well, at the time, I knew that working for a police officer's salary was not going to support my wife and me after my retirement. Also, working hard, fulfilling my family's needs, and making money were ingrained in me at an early age.

Then, the market and economy took a nosedive, which I never saw coming. Long story short, shit happened, and we lost everything—savings account, cars, trucks, boats, motorhome, businesses, all gone. Then, to add insult to injury, the proverbial bankruptcy happened, and we lost our sixty-acre ranch home and four-thousand-foot trailer refurbishing shop, including all the horses and pets.

I'm telling you, if you've never experienced the feeling of not knowing where you're going to move your family to, uprooting them from everything they know, there are just no words to explain how bad it feels. Seriously, I thought about checking out on this one.

There were times on my way to work where I would call my mom and ask her to borrow $7 because that was how much a can of chewing tobacco and a can of diet Mountain Dew cost. That was all I needed to get through the night shift at the time.

So then what? I got the family settled into a townhome in our community, which was very nice, and we felt very blessed and fortunate.

I could have taken all the negative bad fortune and buried my head in the sand, or worse, I could have easily checked out, permanently. But I didn't.

One good thing that I decided back then was to take all those failures and thank God for every step of the journey that my family and I had been through. I was now more determined than ever to continue to succeed in law-enforcement and life.

Being a bit older and somewhat tired at this point, I had to think of something that involved less physical labor for me. By the way, I should say that it was pretty well known throughout the department that my goal was to be an entrepreneur and that I would eventually retire from law-enforcement early. Something my dad said when I was younger that has always stuck with me was, "You're never going to get rich by working for someone else." You have no idea how that sentence has haunted me! I mention this because it's another reason why I worked so hard and always had multiple things going on.

Anyway, back to what happened next: I thought back to my twenties when I took a real estate class with Century 21. I had dabbled in real estate and owned a few income properties back in the day. I decided to get back into the financial fight in 2008 and 2009. I went to school and acquired my real estate license. I passed all the exams on the first attempt. If you remember, back in 2009, there was no real estate market happening, no one was moving, and times were tough. But since I had some experience in the real estate field, I knew that the market would rebound and pick up, and when it did, I wanted to be in the middle of it. When I got my license, I contacted Brian, an acquaintance at the time. Brian was a prominent real estate broker in our community. I knew he and his family were godly people but, at this point, I had no idea how much they would positively impact my life.

Due to the fact, the real estate market was in the toilet, Brian was working another unrelated job out of state. I had told Brian several months before getting my license that I wanted to work with him, and he advised me to call him when that happened. I'm still pretty certain that, to this day, he didn't believe that I would accomplish that task. One of the first things I did after getting my real estate license was to locate a vacant building in our community and rent it. At the time, I had no idea how we were going to afford it, but I didn't care. I was known for taking risks and felt that I was back in the financial game. So, after a good cleanup, a lick of paint, and hanging out an "Open" sign, we were in business.

But 2013 brought more devastation! One of my best friends in the entire world passed away, my mother-in-law (MIL). I won't say much about her death other than she was as good as they came, and she loved Jesus. Her smile and laugh were contagious. The biggest thing she taught me was never to judge anyone, give folks a second chance, and try to spread love as much as possible. My wife and I, and our whole family, miss her terribly to this day.

In addition to real estate, in 2014, my family and I started our own travel business as representatives in a network marketing company. That has been one of the best decisions we have ever made, for many reasons that I will explain later. So, things were once again hectic for me, and I was still refusing to give up.

At this point, I was a full-time cop, a full-time real estate agent, and was running my own network marketing company. If you have never watched the movie *Hollywood Homicide* starring Harrison Ford, check it out; that was my lifestyle for a while. Pretty funny!

This situation continued for quite a while and worked out pretty well. The money was decent, but the old feeling I had back in the nineties was coming back with a vengeance; something in my life was missing. I was making money but had nothing to show for it. It wasn't working. I was firmly stuck in the rat race. Here's a definition of the rat race for you: A way of life in which people are caught up in a fiercely competitive struggle for wealth and power—an exhausting, usually competitive routine.

The more I made, the more I spent. Both the cop and the real estate job became increasingly demanding and time-consuming. I was being pulled in ten different directions. No sleep, no family time, no vacations, plus I was becoming more selfish and feeling sorrier for myself than ever. With that came poor choices. I began a transformation for the worse. I became angry, hateful, and reclusive. I didn't want to do anything with anyone. I just stopped being me. I felt worse than ever. I wasn't the type of person anyone would want to be around. In short, I just wanted to check out.

Thank God for turning points.

CHAPTER 7

The Turning Point

S TILL REFUSING TO give up! I was tired of being sad and dealing with the daily dramas that came along with being a first responder (not to mention the insider politics that goes along with the profession). Sorry, I hope I didn't step on anyone's toes there. It hurts to say, but I no longer loved my chosen profession. If that day ever comes for you, where you no longer love your chosen profession, especially if it's in law enforcement or as a first responder, then my advice is to get out. It's time to consider finding something different to do with your life. I've watched way too many fine officers stay in the profession far too long, and it ruined them. Trust me, staying past your mental or physical prime is not a smart decision or a healthy lifestyle.

What happened next? September 8, 2015, 11:53 am, turned out to be *the* turning point in my life. I was on patrol when my daughter sent me this text message, which no one outside of my family has seen before today. With my daughter's permission, I present it to you word for word:

Sept 8, 2015, 11:53 AM

"But when he asks, he must believe and not doubt, because he who doubts is like a wave of the sea, blown and tossed by the wind."[13]

"If God is for us, who can be against us? He who did not spare us his own son, but gave him up for us all-how will he not also, along with him, graciously give us all things?"[14]

Dad, I've been doing a lot of praying and thinking . . .
God has obviously put quitting the police department on your heart for a long time now.
He's not doing that to torture you.
If it's all you can think about.
If it keeps you up at night and if it makes you sick trying to make the choice, then, in my opinion, that's God telling you to do it.
Take the leap of faith.
Then God is asking you to trust him.
Don't doubt a thing.
God knows that if it's time in your heart that its time.
It might seem risky and it might come with a few scares, hardships and challenges, but dad... It's time.
If God is for us, then who can be against us?
I truly believe now's the time.

---

[13] Jas 1:6 NIV
[14] Rom 8:31-32 NIV

For the sake of your health and your family's health and also,
for the sake of what I believe God has planned for you.
With real estate and WV, God will provide.
He always does. Yes, the world of law-enforcement will be losing
one of the best. But your family and your World Ventures family
will be gaining the best back and I'm so excited for that.
I've been reading Romans a lot lately and I just feel it's time that
I know God will provide and I promise to commit myself to you
and to our business to make this happen for you and mom and
for our family.
It's time daddy. I just really feel it. I love you!

"Be still, and know that I am God."[15]

Yep, that sure got my attention. Has anyone ever hinted to you that it might be time for a change? If so, maybe you should listen. Is it time for your leap of faith?

My daughter got very personal with me and spilled out her heart. That was a courageous thing for her to do because I was not an approachable person back then.

Everything that my daughter said in her text went straight to my core, and I knew it was time for a change. I never felt more at peace in my life than I did the moment after I finished reading her text.

Ironically, later that day, my commander called me into his office to discuss my schedule for the following year. The

---

[15]   Ps. 46:10 NIV

schedules were posted on a whiteboard in his office. He asked me to confirm if I wanted the same schedule for the upcoming year. I found myself staring at the whiteboard for several minutes. Finally, my commander noted my hesitation and asked if I was thinking of changing my schedule. I knew I was stalling, but it was at that moment that I felt my body fill with warmth. I call that the presence of Jesus.

Right then, I knew I had to save my relationship with my family, and I had to fix myself. I finally told my commander that I was giving him a one-week notice. He looked at me and said, "You're f****g kidding!" After we had determined that I was not kidding, he asked if I could stay for two weeks, so he could find my replacement, to which I agreed.

As much as I knew it was time for me to retire from law enforcement, I will tell you it was one of the most difficult decisions I have ever had to make. After all, I loved being a police officer and serving people. I was proud. It was my identity at the time. However, it has been a decision that I have never regretted.

The following two weeks were fantastic because I felt that a new door was opening, one I couldn't wait to go through. My fellow officers, the department staff, firefighters, and medical personnel showed so much affection and gratitude toward me on account of all the things we had been through together as a team.

I had no idea what lay ahead.

Suffice to say that retirement was not at all what I had expected.

CHAPTER 8

The Retirement Journey

ON SEPTEMBER 23, 2015, my agency hosted a wonderful send-off retirement party for me. I'm proud to say that the conference room where we held the gathering was packed with my colleagues. Several of them, including my acting chief and commander, shared some heartfelt, kind words of appreciation for my years of service.

One of the highlights of the gathering was the appearance of the chief who hired me, who showed up to congratulate me. He took a chance in hiring me, but it turned out to be one of his best decisions. That's what I told him anyway during the party, which raised a few chuckles in the room. It was special to see him, especially because he was sick at the time and, unfortunately, passed away about a month later.

My commander also shared a letter with everyone that day, one which my daughter had previously posted on Facebook. I'll share this one with you, as well. Although I knew it well and had read it several times since, I had no idea that they were going to present it at the retirement gathering. It was a great surprise, though.

Dad,

Today is basically the best day ever! A day my family and I have been anticipating for a long time. Today is my dad's last day working in law-enforcement.

He served eighteen rewarding, heroic, and emotional years as a corporal with the police department.

His brothers and sisters in blue are losing an exceptional officer, but his family will be gaining his full presence and attention, and we are so excited. Throughout the past eighteen years, my dad has changed thousands of lives for the better. He has positively affected and also saved many people. He has witnessed horrible things that the average person would be terrified to see. He is a hero to many, but especially to me.

It takes a unique human being to live the everyday life of a police officer. It also takes a special kind of strength to be the wife, mother, daughter, and son of a police officer. I am so grateful that he's able to retire early, especially now with this broken world that we currently live in. He's retiring with humility and grace.

Dad, I'm so proud of you and all of your accomplishments in this world. There's no one quite as magnificent as you. I cannot wait to see what God will unfold in your life. I have a feeling *he's got plenty of vacations, memories, and entrepreneurial successes to be had waiting for us.*

You are an amazing officer, Dad, and an even better person. I could not be prouder and in awe of what you have achieved.

Today and every day, whenever you have the chance, thank a police officer. Buy their coffee, hold the door for them, smile their way. They need and deserve our appreciation. Police officers are heroes; their lives absolutely do matter.

Dad, you're my hero.

I love you. I love you.

Amanda

If you haven't figured it out by now, you can tell that my daughter likes to write, as well.

After my commander read her touching words, I saw a lot of folks with tears in their eyes, including my own. Hearing someone else read it and seeing the effect it had on the audience was heartwarming. I genuinely feel that there were some family members in the audience that day who shared the same feelings my daughter and family had.

After all the kind words that I received, I had the opportunity to read my own retirement speech afterwards. Here is what I said, in its entirety:

> In late 1996, I decided to follow my high school dream of wanting to become a police officer. I started this journey by calling up this police department and asking if there was anyone available, so I could find out how to become a police officer. The captain answered my call and told me that to become a police officer, I would have to take a post-certification class.

> I had no idea the journey I was about to embark on. At this time, my wife and I were both in our thirties with children, my daughter was nine while my son was five. I began my eleven-month course and obtained the post-certification at the end of it. After I received it, I then called the captain again, and he recommended that I become a reserve police officer, which I did.

> I did that for a while and by June 1998 I was asked if I wanted to become a dispatcher, which I agreed to. That's when I learned that you had to be a special and talented individual for that position. I found out quickly that the job was a multitasking nightmare, and you had to be both incredibly patient and dedicated. Thank you, dispatchers, for keeping me safe all those years, I love you guys.

After becoming a dispatcher, I continued to study for a police officer position and took the next available test. When that test came along, I was beaten out by a guy that you all know. So, I retook the test and, in November 1998, I fulfilled my dream and got sworn in as a full-time police officer. Another officer and I were both sworn in the same day, and we were sworn-in inside a small broom closet because that was the only space available at that time.

Once sworn in, I found out quickly that the post-certification academy had failed to tell me something very important, which was this: No one told me that while becoming a police officer, I was also required to be a social worker, a family psychologist, a child psychologist, a doctor, a nurse, a criminal lawyer, a civil lawyer, an assistant coroner, an animal control officer, and the parent to other peoples' children.

On top of all those different hats that we must wear, I found that I also needed to be a comedian because I discovered that always helped me with getting through the day. And as if this wasn't enough, I also needed to be a parent to my own kids, a husband, a son, a brother, an uncle, a cousin, a friend, an in-law, a nephew, and a superior employee.

Another thing no one had told me was how difficult shift work could be, and no one told me how many holidays, kid events, and family functions I would end up missing throughout the *years. With that being said, thank you to my wife and kids who have stuck with me through thick and thin. Officers, hug all your family members and assure them that you are okay, because this profession is hard on them, as well.*

While being all the things expected of us, we must remain calm, happy, positive, strong, smile, humble, faithful, and, if possible, try not to make anyone mad along the way. Why? Because that's what's expected of us.

I say all of this because what you all do, as commanders, investigators, patrol supervisors, patrol officers, dispatchers, and victim advocates, records clerk's, court clerks, and all other police civilians is hard, but this hard work and your dedication does not go unrecognized or unappreciated, even though it feels like it does sometimes.

We are police officers and do what we do with pride, dignity, integrity, and honor, and we are willing to make many sacrifices, because we believe in our chosen profession. We truly believe we can make a difference in someone's life.

Without police officers, the world would be chaos. Thank you for allowing me to train most of you and be trained by a lot of you, as well.

In closing, I never met a more dedicated group of people who have the same goals of making this police department great. I've been blessed to have served this police department, this community, and this entire organization.

I'm very proud of my time here. It's now time for my family and me to enjoy a simpler life. I have had an entrepreneurial spirit for years, and it is now time for me to follow this dream.

Thank you all for what you do. It has truly been an honor of working with you all.

Please be safe and, if you ever need anything, just ask.

God bless you all.

Thank you

After reading these words to the audience, it fully sank in that my decision to retire early was for the best. Following the gathering, my family and I went out and celebrated with a nice dinner. I realized that evening, I did not have to set my alarm clock for the next day or any other day if I didn't want to. I must admit, it felt great.

I am grateful that I had the opportunity of working for the agency that I did. I would put that agency up against any agency in the state of Colorado. The men and women that work there were, and still are, the best of the best. It was truly an honor.

I ended my career as a patrol corporal, which was the best position in the department as far as I'm concerned. It was a supervisory role, but I still got to work in the trenches with my team. People often ask me if I had known then what I know now, would I still have become a police officer? My answer has always been and will always remain, yes. I believe it was a crucial part of my journey of making me the man that I am today.

I also ended my career not knowing that the next few years of my life were going to be the most difficult and challenging ones, but, having survived them, I am sure that it was all worth it.

There you have it: Badge # 98-05 was officially retired.

Stay tuned; I couldn't have made it without Backup.

CHAPTER 9

After the Beat

NOW IS WHERE I start my story about rising after the beat. It was the point where I found myself with no job, no income, few savings, and no real estate deal anywhere in sight.

The next few years after retirement sucked the most. Let me explain how it started. I quickly found out that all the power and authority I had while on duty, supervisor (or not), no longer existed. I later found out that most retired cops called this their "Identity Crisis." I discovered quickly after retiring that I was no longer one of the most popular guys around. Earlier, whenever I used to walk into a room or a restaurant, it was amazing the attention that the uniform attracted. It made me seem more attractive than I was. I went downhill from being at the top of my game to not having one. I lost whatever purpose I thought I had and my sense of importance, or so I thought.

For the first month and a half or so after retiring, I did absolutely nothing and barely even left the house. I felt exhausted, unmotivated, and a little lost. I guess I was bored with the monotonous life. It was because I was used to so much structure back in my day, with everybody always telling me what to do.

People had my schedule laid out for me, and the only thing I had to do was show up on time and perform my duties.

So, I found myself still living the life of the swing shift schedule. I stayed up till two or three every morning, staring at the TV with the volume down because I didn't want to wake up my wife. But there was nothing on the TV I wanted to particularly see. Pretty mindless, huh! The TV irritated the living shit out of me, and I had a negative remark for every commercial. But I especially hated the news.

I realize now that I was forming some pretty unhealthy habits during that time. I had to wait to go to bed until I was physically exhausted. I felt nauseous often. If I didn't do that, I would simply lie down and watch the clock for hours upon hours, reminiscing about my police career, constantly seeing myself in uniform. I would replay the calls for service in my head. Typically, the calls would involve dead children, either dead by suicide or at the hands of their parents. Also, when I was finally able to go to bed, I would close my eyes, and the first thing that I would visualize would be those red and blue flashing overhead patrol car lights. It's incredible how bright those lights appear at night. It took some time for that image to wear off. I couldn't understand why all this was happening, because I knew I didn't want to go back into law enforcement, so what was the possible explanation?

Another habit that I carried over from active duty was never to stop counting my fingers—both hands and in perfect unison. I did recognize this behavior when I was on duty and so did a few of my partners. It typically occurred when I was in a nerve-racking situation or on standby prior to a tense situation. I never thought much of it back then, considering it as some kind of stress release, which turned into a nervous habit that I thought I could stop at any time utilizing my will power. I can only explain it as being something like a nervous leg shake when somebody is being interviewed for a job. After retirement, I noticed that the finger counting persisted, especially when I went to bed because that's when my brain could not shut its long history and association with law enforcement. It was so bad at times that often, during the middle of the night, my wife would wake up and ask me to stop because I was touching her and the movement disturbed her sleep.

When I did fall asleep, it would only be for a short time, a few hours at a time, and even then, I was extremely restless. That was also due to the nightmares I often experienced. I was fighting somebody or chasing after them in these dreams. When the fights ensued, it was horrible and, unfortunately, I acted them out in my sleep. My poor wife was on the receiving end of it all. She shared a story with me about one night where I was sitting on top of her getting ready to punch her in the face. She said she had to scream several times to make me stop.

Then there was the time when I woke up in the morning to find things knocked over and a broken lamp, which (as my wife later explained to me) I had done during the middle of the night.

I can only vaguely recall those incidents, but I know that these were ongoing and recurring problems.

It eventually got so bad that I started sleeping in a different room because I was fearful of hurting my wife. I would stay in bed for most of the day and repeated the same nightly routine over and over, caught in some loop.

I will admit that there were times when I was ready to check out permanently, but, at that point, it had become more than just a threat to my mental health, and I began thinking about checking out more often. I used to get mad at myself and felt like a hypocrite because I remembered how I felt when I was on duty investigating suicide calls. It made me angry, and I always felt that the person involved was selfish. I thought the folks who suffered more were the loved ones left behind. I knew I couldn't do anything like that to my family, but I had to convince myself that taking my life was not an option, although it sure did consume my thoughts at the time.

Up to this point, my wife had been extremely patient and had never really said a whole lot about how she was feeling, but I knew that the situation wasn't healthy for her either. I could see it on her face and in her posture. I noticed it, but I didn't care at that point, and I couldn't talk with her or anyone else for that matter. She finally came to her breaking point one night and just melted. She told me that she was never going to give up on me, but she didn't want to live that way any longer. She pretty much spilled her guts, and we reviewed our lives together. It was the first time that I had been up for any type of discussion, but seeing her so upset did not sit well with me.

Her biggest request was to ask me to spend more time talking with God and asking Him for his help, to trust Him, and stop doubting him. She also basically told me to pick up my big boy pants and get my ass back to work, because we were out of money and the debt was piling up. She was tired, and I could see that. I saw myself as an extreme failure and a loser. I recall distinctly telling her when I asked her to marry me that I would give her everything she ever wanted and that she would never regret the choice she made when agreeing to marry me. Yep, I felt like a failure and pretty much wanted to check out again. I did not take it lightly.

But that conversation also struck a spark in me that I can't explain. I knew that I had to fix the situation—again. The first thing I did was to get down on my knees and pray to God for help. I begged God for His forgiveness for all the years of my life that I had wasted in sin. God and I had some serious conversations. I knew I had doubted Him way too much, but now we were at least on talking terms. This was also one of those huge, proverbial turning points in my life. Thank God! But I was still very emotionally confused and wasn't at all sure that I wanted to go on living.

Like they say onward and upward, always. Do you remember Brian? I joined his real estate company and started an office with him in 2009. We started as mere acquaintances, but he's more like a brother to me now than a business partner. I forgot to mention that he is also a pastor of a well-known church in our community. Let's just say that, unbeknownst to him, Brian literally saved my life.

I called Brian the next day after having that very long talk with my wife about our lives together. I still call that talk with my wife, one of the best ass-chewings I have ever received from her.

Brian and I met up and discussed my situation, and he was incredibly supportive. He shared some personal things about his own life, and quoted words from the Bible, which were extraordinarily motivational and helpful. He told me that everything would be alright if I trusted God and didn't doubt Him anymore. That hit very close to home because God and I had that conversation recently.

Brian recommended I start reading the following:

1. John 19—Jesus Delivered to Be Crucified
2. Romans—whose theme deals with the revelation of God's judgment and saving righteousness on the cross of Christ, and His justice and mercy
3. Psalm 1—The Way of the Righteous and the Wicked
4. Psalm 18—The Lord Is My Rock and My Fortress
5. Psalm 32—Blessed Are the Forgiven
6. Psalm 34—Taste and See That the Lord Is Good
7. Psalm 51—Create in Me a Clean Heart, O God
8. Psalm 103—Bless the Lord, O My Soul
9. Psalm 130—My Soul Waits for the Lord (Which I Did)

It was as though Brian knew what I was feeling and had hand-picked each of those sections from the scriptures specifically for me, as I needed to hear those messages to begin my healing process. That was when I started to listen, instead of always being in control and doing all the talking. I highly recommend reading these scriptures. Remember, I also mentioned earlier that Brian never really knew he saved my life, but that was the day he did, with God's help. Brian had no idea that I was contemplating taking my life that day. I remember him telling me that God and he would always have my back. Those were the first major words of encouragement I received from anybody, other than my wife and children, after I retired. That day spent with Brian taught me a precious lesson- to always consider other people's feelings. Whoever crosses your path, even if they are mean, always keep in mind that they may be going through certain issues themselves. You never know if they might need a word of encouragement, as well.

After visiting Brian that day, I prayed harder than I've ever prayed in my life and decided that my lifestyle was unhealthy for me and the people around me. That same day, I decided to start fresh. The first thing that I felt God told me to do was to start taking care of myself. I forced myself to do a thirty-minute treadmill workout and found it extremely helpful. I felt that exercise actually made me feel better about myself, and it also got my mind working again. It helped me to get my entrepreneurial juices flowing again.

In the words of Jim Carrey:

> "I believe depression is legitimate. But I also believe that if you don't exercise, eat nutritious foods, get sunlight, get enough sleep, consume positive material, and surround yourself with support, then you aren't giving yourself a fighting chance."[16]

After the workout, I started making some phone calls for both my real estate business and my network marketing company. I was ready to get back out in public and start socializing again.

For the most part, things were starting to flow again, and I was getting back into a routine. But just a few days after that, I had an unexpected and, at that time, unexplainable setback.

My wife and I went to a Lowe's store in the city where I used to patrol. We were looking at appliances. This was one of my first outings after retiring. I specifically recall that we were walking down an aisle holding hands when there was an announcement over the loudspeaker intercom. It was very similar to the law enforcement alert tone prior to a hot call for service. Then a female voice stated: "Code ten, register four." Remember, we discussed Code Ten in chapter five? Code Ten means (in law-enforcement terms) that, somewhere, the shit was hitting the fan. It was more than likely that an officer was in trouble and

16 Kristan Buck, "Belles & Bucks," *Belles & Bucks* (blog) (Kristan Buck, July 18, 2019), https://www.bellesandbucks.com/depression-mindset-matters/.

needed help immediately! Well, of all places to be after being out of law enforcement, this is where it had to rear its ugly head.

After the loudspeaker intercom announcement, I could immediately feel my body starting to heat up from the inside out. My arms and legs began to feel heavy, to the point where I couldn't physically walk. My face went numb and I started sweating profusely. I also felt extremely nauseous and belched like crazy. I had a hard time catching my breath. I had no idea what the hell was happening. No one had ever told me that this could also happen. I do remember my wife starting to panic and asking me several times if I was okay, but I couldn't physically answer her. I instantly looked for a place to hide and wedged myself in between two refrigerators. Then, my entire career right from the time I was sworn in, from the broom closet through almost every horrible call for service I had ever taken flashed before my eyes as if all of that was happening at that moment. It was all very detailed, and I felt like it was happening all over again. It was like an old slideshow projector clicking through my mind. I was crying uncontrollably.

My wife later told me that this incident lasted for about thirty minutes before I was able to communicate with her and finally give up my safe space between the refrigerators. I'm so grateful that my wife was with me that day. She just stood there, blocking me from the public view and protected me the whole time. Trust me, she had no idea what the hell was happening, either. Believe it or not, I don't care, but that's what happened.

Can anyone relate? Boy, did this effect piss me off? It seemed as though I had zero control over my mind, body, and emotions.

After recovering somewhat, my wife and I immediately left the store and headed back home. I later explained to her what I had experienced, and we left it at that. For the next two days, I felt as if I was recovering from a major hangover. I stayed in bed for a couple of days.

On the third day or so, I knew that I couldn't just give up. I forced my happy ass back on to that damned dreaded treadmill and decided to fight again.

From that day forward, I started plugging into life again and started getting back out in public. Between my real estate business and my network marketing organization, I have had some fantastic mentors, friends, and business partners, and I began surrounding myself with them. I would go to meetings and attend as many events as possible. However, I always sat in the back of the room, so I could be close to the exit and monitor who came in and out of the room. These events and those people were all lifesavers, too, and they never even knew it. They had no idea what was going on in my life at that time. The people surrounding me were some of the most positive and supportive people I have ever met, and we all share the same entrepreneur life mindset.

Trust me on this one, if you ever find yourself in a bad place, then the best thing to do is to surround yourself with leaders and influencers. These people support you for all the right reasons. The Christian group Casting Crowns came out with a song called *Just Be Held*. There is a verse that says: "You're not alone, stop holding on and just be held. Your world's not falling apart, it's falling into place."[17] I trusted that verse and listened to that song a hundred times on loop during that period of my life.

So, by the grace of God and a lot of prayers, some real estate deals started to come in my way, and our network marketing business also started to grow.

I was still searching for what my exact purpose was in life, and I was still experiencing some unexplainable symptoms that I could not quite shake. I was still a work in progress.

I believe that until you find your purpose in life, your life will not change until your purpose is well defined in your mind. I also believe that knowing God and making Him known is also the purpose of the believer.

So, here are some examples of those unexplainable symptoms: Any loud noises or familiar high-pitched loud tones would put me right back into that sweaty, nauseous, and hard-to-breathe state and into the slideshow projection of my career. Any sirens that I didn't see prior to hearing them would generate the same effect, including any traffic accidents that I had to pass through. The highly realistic nightmares continued as though events were happening all over again. I had to completely eliminate the news channels from my life because the news reminded me of the low points of my career. It focused too much on police action and was always typically negative. These things continued well

---

17 Casting Crowns, "Just Be Held," 2015, track 7 on *A Live Worship Experience*, Beach Street / Reunion, 2015, compact disc

into my third and fourth years of retirement. Unfortunately, they continue to haunt me even today but, thankfully, less frequently. I'm now able to fight through these effects and control how long they last. The duration of the episodes continue to get reduced with fewer physical aftereffects.

So, after approximately four years of retirement, what had changed? Why did I think I was feeling better? Well, for one thing, I started to get really pissed-off and angry about the way these aftereffects controlled my life and also affected my family. I decided to be extremely stubborn. I was going to fight like hell until I had finally won the war. So, every time the negative trigger effect started, I told myself I wasn't going to let it happen and would continually repeat that in my head. The effects would still start, but I would try to think of something positive or happy, typically about our Lake Powell vacations with my family and friends or the time I had spent with my granddaughter, who joined our family in May 2017. I cannot explain how positively this tiny girl has impacted my life but I'm so grateful for her. My granddaughter makes me a better person.

My counter-actions began to work on my mind, so I was able to shorten the slideshow effect by what I called self-talk. These days, I've got it down to where such attacks happen rarely. But they happened pretty frequently for the first two-plus years of retirement, occurring less frequently over the following years. I've now got it narrowed down to experiencing just the initial onset of nausea and belching while keeping the slideshow effect to a minimum. The attacks no longer last for three days; I can usually get past them in about thirty minutes or so. It's still a work in progress, but it's quite manageable. I will continue to fight and pray that someday these effects will completely go away.

Please keep in mind that I'm not telling you this to gain any sympathy. I do not need any recognition. This is not the purpose of this story. I've already lived through it and kicked its ass! I am sharing what happened to me and my family solely to let you know and make you aware that if something like this does happen to you, you and your loved ones have an armor of defense. There is some hope. You can get through it. Fight it as if your life depends on it because it just might.

I will confess, immediately after leaving law-enforcement, my wife and I contacted only one counselor regarding my feelings. This counselor made us feel like a number. It was probably one of the most uncomfortable conversations I've ever had. I didn't enjoy it at all. However, the seed was planted that day when I showed the beginning signs of PTSD. I also decided never to meet with another counselor ever again. That's how bad that meeting was.

Being the strong-headed, retired cop and controlling type of guy that I was and coming from law-enforcement, where a good chunk of my CIT citizens had PTSD, I didn't buy what that counselor was selling. Within law enforcement, that type of announcement would raise a lot of eyebrows, and you didn't want to appear weak in front of your peers, especially not as a supervisor. It's not good to show weakness, right? Wrong! Get your ass in and talk with someone. Most agencies are good at supplying referrals these days, and, if you're retired, do it for yourself and your family. Find someone who is a good fit for you, as I managed to do later, which you can read about in the next chapter.

My wife and I never discussed that first counseling meeting. I convinced myself that that kind of thing could never happen to me. I probably should've looked into it a little bit more, don't you think?

If you ever experience or have experienced anything as I did, then fight. Do not, I repeat, do not check out. Ask for help. We can always do more together than we can accomplish by ourselves. People are counting on you.

I will talk more about the fight in the final chapter.

Now, let's hear from some other first responders and get their perspectives.

CHAPTER 10

A Licensed Counselor Shares Her Perspective

I N THIS CHAPTER, a licensed professional counselor gives us her perspective of the story in chapter nine when I had that first attack in the store with my wife. Was I going crazy, was it normal, was I making that shit up, and should I have asked for professional help instead of fighting through it on my own? I needed some validation to wrap things up. Let's see how it turned out.

A week or so prior to January 28, 2020, I made an appointment with Shauna, a licensed professional counselor, who I had first met back in 2000. She was a dispatcher for my department and served with us for four years prior to leaving. After she left, unfortunately, we did not stay in touch. But that June, our paths crossed again.

Around the beginning of that June, I had an unfortunate verbal argument with a family member over what I call a misunderstanding. Admittedly, I used my PTSD as an excuse, and it backfired on me.

BACKUP AFTER THE BEAT

During this argument, a family member challenged the existence of PTSD, which I'm thankful for today, because that's why I have never again used PTSD as an excuse for anything or referred to it in a conversation with someone who might not understand it. I'm a bit protective of folks who battle PTSD.

Anyway, it pissed me off, so I did something I had never done before, I ranted on Facebook. I have never ranted on Facebook since.

Here's what my ranting post said:

> *PTSD—Well, here's my first post ever and I'm only speaking of it because it is a tough one, and something several folks and I work with every day, in some instances, all the time.*

> *While in law enforcement, I witnessed a lot of things most folks would not want to see.*

> *I worked with a lot of folks dealing with PTSD, mind you, I'm not an expert in this field at all, but it is not something to take lightly.*

> *Some folks work hard dealing with this daily.*

> *Some folks deal with it on an occasional basis when it rears its nasty little head.*

This typically comes around when a bad memory or a certain sound arises or when folks become scared in fear of something, and then that suddenly turns into anger and possibly rage.

It is very, very hard to control, only speaking for myself.

The moral of this story is that I pray for folks who are working through PTSD.

Talk with your loved ones about it, so that they can understand what it is that really happens to you.

If you know someone with PTSD, my only advice would be to take the time to understand it and have a bit of patience.

If someone ever tells you that PTSD is a "pitiful excuse," ignore them, and it's probably not a bad idea to eliminate them from your contact.

Once again, I pray for you all and keep working through things.

There are people that care.

Please do not respond to this post, but feel free to email me.

God Bless!

I am very thankful for that verbal argument with my family member and being called out for blaming PTSD. If not for that argument, the next thing that happened may not have ever come to fruition. Thankfully, this family member and I salvaged our relationship. I'm grateful to them to this day for having the courage to confront me about what they strongly felt was the right thing for them to do. Nothing but respect!

I mention this because, after the ranting Facebook post, Shauna responded out of nowhere. She supplied me with information, and her reaching out felt encouraging and supportive. I also learned that Shauna was now a licensed counselor.

Shauna was one of only a few people who responded to that ranting post, either via email, a phone call, or through Facebook, which I thought was unfortunate.

I just think that some people don't believe that PTSD is a real thing, or they are afraid of the PTSD topic. I say that because, when I was still on duty, I sometimes questioned if PTSD was a real thing. Was it an excuse for bad behavior, being sad, or the "poor me" thing, or was it a way to escape reality? I'm here to tell you that it's real, and it's a real pain in the ass.

In January 2020, I reached out to Shauna, and she immediately called me back and made an appointment to see me a few days later. It was a long weekend, and I did not sleep much in anticipation of the meeting. On the morning of the appointment, I emailed chapter nine to Shauna so that she would have time to read it prior to my arrival. I did not figure out why this meeting weighed so heavily on me until I was driving to her office that day. I felt as though I was going to get the answer as to whether I actually had PTSD or if I was just crazy. Was I the only person in the world that these types of things ever happened to? It sure felt like it. It had turned around on me; was I visiting Shauna for her perspective on chapter nine, or was I looking for an explanation of me? Needless to say, I was very nervous.

Upon arrival at Shauna's office, she greeted me with a hug, and I have to admit it was really good to see her. Her office was small but felt very comfortable. She made me feel welcome, which is not what

happened the only other time I met with a counselor after retiring. Unfortunately, that first meeting had left a horrible taste in my mouth about the counseling profession, but Shauna and I got started on the right foot. We started talking about our families and how and why she got into her profession and how I got to where I was at that time. It was just a casual conversation catching up since we'd last had contact with each other. It did not take long before the nervousness went away. The small talk led us to discuss chapter nine. We talked about a lot, and she even got me to speak in detail about a time that I took a substantial step toward ending my own life.

Shauna had more to say about her thoughts and perspective, but here's what I remember most about what she said during that first meeting. She told me that what I was experiencing was normal, and I was not the only one in the world who had experienced the adverse trigger effects described in chapter nine. She said that my brain had suffered trauma from everything that

I'd seen in my law enforcement career, and those bad memories had left imprints. She advised me that I did indeed have PTSD, and firmly stated, "Steve, you're not crazy!"

When Shauna said that, I immediately felt all the air leave my body, and I just dropped my head. Tears started to pour out. I felt so relieved that I finally knew the truth about what had been haunting me. Just knowing that it was normal helped. Shauna said it was okay not to be okay, and that made perfect sense to me. She also stated that she was proud of me for hanging in there and fighting it as well as I had without any counseling. But, and you can trust me on this, I should have gotten help long before then.

After our meeting, Shauna and I agreed to meet again soon. When I left her office and started walking towards my truck, I immediately felt like the weight of the world had been lifted off my shoulders. I felt the validation Shauna gave me and felt things were going to be okay. Mind you, prior to that day, I had felt I was slowly winning the fight against PTSD, but after our meeting, I felt more confident about actually beating it in the long-term.

So, please listen when I say, go and talk to someone and get help!

On January 29th, 2020, Shauna emailed me her perspectives. Here is what Shauna wrote:

I knew Steve Eastin when I was a dispatcher, and he was a cop working at the same agency from 2000—2004. During those years, I saw him as a reliable, trustworthy, kind, and an overall really good guy. He's the one you would want to respond to your house if there was an emergency. I have always looked up to Steve. Fast forward fifteen years and a new career as a licensed professional counselor, when he reached out to me to get a professional perspective on his struggles after retirement.

"I read a previous chapter that he had written and met with him for a little over an hour, so the following will be more than my professional opinion, as I am unable to separate my personal feelings from my professional ideas in this case.

Steve previously said that as a police officer, he felt that he was connected, well respected, and had overall meaning associated with all the tragedy he had to encounter. If he saw something horrible, he could put it on a shelf, and the perks of the job were enough to keep those things on the shelf. Additionally, the department did not encourage counseling or have good debriefings. And resiliency training was not even talked about. Police officers have historically been set up to have problems.

When I had a chance to read Steve's chapter and speak to him, I heard how retirement left him disconnected from all the previous people and activities that used to offer him support. Those horrible things that used to be sitting on the shelf were suddenly rearing their ugly heads. And, since Steve was never warned about the adverse effects that could occur, he was caught off guard by how hard it can be to cope with them.

What Steve describes are symptoms of PTSD. You can also call them symptoms of stress injuries or trauma injuries. They are a normal response to being constantly exposed to horrific things without the means to process them.

Steve then started to describe to me the things he has done to help decrease his symptoms and attempt to put the past in the past. He talked about his deeper connection with his faith, supportive family members, and supportive friends. He spoke about building businesses, his successes, and redirecting his negative thoughts. And finally, he talked about writing his story. All these things are very effective strategies that have sent him down the road to recovery. He has excellent insight and self-awareness, and his desire to share his story and be vulnerable has only deepened my admiration for him. He is still the really good guy I knew all those years ago.

My only recommendation for Steve is that if things seem to stop going in an upward direction, he seeks help from a professional

A LICENSED COUNSELOR SHARES HER PERSPECTIVE

who specializes in helping first responders. Preferably a professional who utilizes EMDR (Eye Movement Desensitization and Reprocessing). It is a trauma-specific therapy that can speed up the healing process. For more information, you can use this link: https://www.emdria.org.

Steve highlights the need for better resources before, during, and after public service. The old-school mentality is killing people. I hope Steve's story gives someone else the courage to be vulnerable and ask for help. I hope that people will learn that it is okay not to be okay."

I cannot tell you how grateful I am to Shauna. I feel that she has brought me closer to having closure in the life-chapter of PTSD. After speaking with Shauna, I truly felt that this book has a purpose, and that purpose is to touch and save lives. I want people to know that it's okay to have PTSD and to talk about it openly. People should not be afraid to talk about PTSD. PTSD is not something to be ashamed of; it happens to the best of us.

It's more than likely going to be with me for life, but, as Shauna said during my conversation with her, to just let it run through you but know it will not win. It's like a headache, it sucks while it's happening, but it will be fine once it goes away. It will get easier, so hang in there.

CHAPTER 11

My Children's Perspective of Growing up with a Cop Dad

I ASKED MY DAUGHTER, Amanda, and son, Danny, whether they would be willing to provide their perspective on being the daughter and son of a police officer. They agreed – although my son said that he would relay his two cents' worth to my daughter. He is quiet in nature, but this does not prevent him from being one of my main go-to guys! Both of my children would do anything to help someone out and words cannot explain how proud I am of the people they are today. They were beautiful from day one.

I received their story on January 30, 2020, and this is what they had to say:

> My dad entered the police academy late in life, as some might say. He was thirty then. My brother was two or three, I think, and I was six or seven. Growing up as a police officer's child wasn't anything like most people think it is. I think many people assume that having a dad who's a cop would make your childhood rather strict or cause you to rebel for the sake

of rebellion. It wasn't bad at all, much like being the child of a pastor.

My childhood felt breezy and normal because I wasn't a menace to society. I never got into any real trouble, never attended house parties, never partook in any drinking or drugs - not even weed, until later in life as an adult. Such a goody-two-shoes, right? Although some things were tempting - seeing that barn shindigs and cow tipping while under the influence of far too much Coors Light was a thing in our town. Yet, I just didn't participate. I was (and still am) a homebody. I dated and married a homeschooled kid. As I was growing up, I enjoyed the solace of home and never really left the house, except for sports.

As kids, we lived in the sticks, far out in the plains. Maybe living in such a way kept my brother and I out of mischief - not only with our parents but with the law as well. Or maybe it was just that we were scared to death of messing up: having a cop for a father could have meant a VIP ticket straight to the big house. So, we laid low. Do I regret not "living a little" in my high school days? Not really. Though we were scared of getting into trouble, I don't think we necessarily felt suffocated either. There were times in life when I didn't feel encouraged to grow up but looking back now, I realize that probably my dad had seen first-hand how kids were ending up and didn't want that outcome for my brother and I. Now that I'm a mom, I can understand that. Did I ever think that, should the opportunity arise, I could get myself out of a speeding ticket with a simple name-drop? Heck yes! It even worked once or twice.

We were fortunate to have a stay-at-home mom. Had my mother also worked, things probably would have been a whole lot different. Home-life with my mom was always good and comfortable. We had near-and-dear cousins who were close in age to us and they were over nearly every weekend for playing and sleepovers. Though dad wasn't always present on Christmas day, the holiday itself was always magical, and we were well cared for—spoiled, really. We simply made sure we celebrated on a day when dad was home. Every year, we also enjoyed a family vacation to Lake Powell and always made sweet memories. For this trip, my dad always took time off work; there were absolutely no exceptions when it came to Lake Powell. Even today, that little slice of heaven is my haven; my safe place, as it is my dad's. Those summers, every single one of those trips, are engraved on my mind forever.

If you were to ask my little brother, he would probably agree with all these things. I do think, though, that my dad's absence at events like wrestling meets and baseball games were a bit harder on him than it was on me. When dad came home after his four-day shift, our routine would shift a little too. Yet, we were always glad to have him home alive and safe in our midst for another week. Probably the two hardest things I dealt with as a police officer's child were:

1. Seeing my mom worry as she did, although I must say that she concealed her emotions pretty well. In all honesty, I'm not sure whether she's slept in the last twenty-odd years.

2. Having to be ever so quiet during the day while dad slept off the graveyard shift. That was pretty tough, especially when the cousins came over. We compensated by playing outside a lot, a true advantage of living in the country.

Being the daughter of a cop came with its perks, too. No boy was ever going to mess with me. Bless my husband's heart for dating me with such ease and grace! Especially for asking my dad if he could marry me while riding a shift in the patrol car, knowing full well my dad was packing! What a brave thing to do at just twenty years of age. Another perk was that I got to prance around, exclaiming that my dad was a real-life superhero who protected and saved lives every day. Even now, as a thirty-something woman, I'll grab any chance to proudly say that my dad is a retired police hero of eighteen years. All in all, we lived a joyful childhood, and that's the only way I remember it.

The real hardships for me, personally, came with his retirement. Don't get me wrong! I was elated that he finally left the force. I'm the one who begged and pleaded for him to leave. I wrote him an emotional letter and painted this picture of what life would be like once he was free. That was in 2015 when it seemed as if the world was becoming an increasingly dangerous mire. I just didn't want him immersing himself in that danger any longer. My words struck a chord, and he quit on the spot. He retired without any warning.

I'm grateful that he did this. Nowadays you can't turn on the TV or scroll through Facebook without seeing tragic news about another officer's life that has been taken unfairly. Being a police officer is a noble profession. Policemen and firefighters, all first responders alike, they are genuine heroes who don't receive enough recognition. I commend and honor each of them and their families, their spouses and partners especially. If you are reading this and you fall into this category, I thank you for your service and I pray for you every day.

With my dad's retirement, the force lost a true asset. In our personal lives, retirement was accompanied with one little problem: PTSD. She's an ugly bitch. I used to think it was bogus, a selfish ploy to escape real life or cover up the fact that you're actually a jerk. I wish I had been right. I never noticed my dad's PTSD as a child. I think if you were to ask my brother, he might say something different. Possibly, that could be a difference between being the son or the daughter of a cop, or the consequence of being the younger sibling.

It wasn't until about two years after his retirement that I came face to face with the brutality of PTSD. It's a story that is intensely personal to my family and myself and does not need a whole lot of highlighting. What happened, broke me. It took me almost a year or so to get over this life-altering event. It may even be the reason why I suffer from a bit of my own PTSD today.

What happened in my family on that fateful day - May 27, 2017 - gave me vast insight into PTSD. I realized how it can affect a human being who has experienced several traumatic events in their life and how it can debut itself in unexpected ways. I wish there were a cure, a pill you could take as a quick fix to make all the hurt go away. As for the aftermath of an episode and the temporary destruction it causes, I wish I could have popped a pill for that too. Unfortunately, it was (and still is) a healing process that love and Jesus alone have pulled us through.

What happened that day in May might not seem like a big deal to most, but to me, it was. At first, I was mad. So mad that I thought the anger and disappointment might physically kill me. I held onto resentment for longer than my dad might even know and longer than I care to admit. It took a fusion of three specific events for me to see life through my dad's eyes and truly empathize with the heartache that goes hand-in-hand with battling symptoms of PTSD, especially after retirement. I'd like to break these events down for you one by one so that the way it all came together and my strengthened love for my dad makes sense. I love my dad more than I can say in mere words.

The first event that helped me understand my dad better, happened at Lake Powell of all places. It was a trip that just my dad and I took, one of many. As mentioned before, it's our safe haven and something we share a bond of understanding over. We had my then eighteen-month-old baby girl in tow. We were in the truck, driving circles around the lake to try and get her to take a much-needed car nap. This gave us a lot of time to talk. I'm not sure what we were talking about but, out of nowhere, my dad started speaking of a specific call for service he went out on. During this call, he got the opportunity to arrest a man he'd been pursuing for months—a man who had been sexually abusing his young daughter. My dad talked about it as if it didn't really bother him, but as I listened I realized that deep pain was oozing from his heart while he remembered the details. He shared quite a lot with me and before I knew it, I was sobbing. Grotesque pictures flashed through my head of what I imagined that little girl had gone through, and I couldn't contain myself. That night, I had nightmares about something I hadn't ever experienced. It was at that moment that I gained palpable understanding and could grasp just a sliver of the things my dad had seen.

The second event happened months later when again, just my dad and I were driving in his truck. I think we were driving home from Lake Powell through the mountains in a rough snowstorm after a spring break trip to the lake. You see, for healing and hope to occur, just go to Lake Powell, Utah! Anyway, the snow was coming down and if you're a Colorado native, you know how dreadful the I-70 can be in the winter. A severe accident took place just in front of us. Before we knew it, police cars, fire trucks, and ambulances were surrounding us. At first, my dad was silent. Then heavy breathing, belching, and a balmy whiteness in his face kicked in. I realized he was having a panic attack, a PTSD-related episode that had been triggered by the red and blue of the flashing lights and the loud cry of the sirens. I had nothing but empathy for him at that moment. My heart softened and opened a little more.

The third event happened just weeks ago, as I write this. A well-known man in our small community died tragically and unexpectedly. A close friend of mine, who is a new fireman, was first on scene for the accident. Not just first on the scene of a death, but first on the scene of the death of a close friend of his. When I heard the news, I was bereaved for this young man and, of course, for his family. But I also felt a tremendous amount of heartbreak for my friend, the fireman, who had to experience this. How then could I offer grace and condolences to my friend for what he had witnessed but not for my dad, with the many terrors he must have seen and experienced over his eighteen years in service? It finally dawned on me that no one can ever prepare you for what you will see in eighteen years or even one year as a police officer, firefighter, or first responder. No one. And no one can ever prepare you for how you should handle it. Even if you think you're strong enough, macho enough, or emotionless enough to handle such things, you're still a human being with a beating, sensitive heart. That stuff just sits with you, forever.

I've held onto a lot in the last few years, all while drudging through the trenches of postpartum depression, along with all that comes with being a new mom. Let me tell you, it's been super glamorous. But with PPD or PTSD, or any mental struggle really, it's okay to not always be okay. It's okay to take the time you need to heal and, if you're lucky enough to have a supportive family, then forgiveness and understanding will come. Grace is important, and love always wins.

I've been cold. And some days, I still struggle. Dad, just like this book is your way of standing up to PTSD and telling it to go to hell while closing the hard but heroic law enforcement chapter of your life; this chapter is my way of saying that I forgive you. I revere you. I treasure you, and I understand you. You're a strong human being and one hell of a man. You're often stubborn and sassy, but now I know where both your granddaughter and I get it from!

I can't imagine the valleys you've walked through; no one besides you can ever really know or fully understand. I do know the mountains you've conquered and stood upon, though, because countless people praise the work you did and the difference you made while on the force. I am one of them.

I apologize for all the times I didn't understand what you were battling. I hope you can forgive me for the distance I allowed to creep in between us when I was dealing with my own demons. Even if you didn't feel it, I did. I'm grateful we can laugh about it now. We are a stronger father-daughter team because of it.

And now, even though we can't attend a big event without you having to sit on the end seat of the back row (can any other retired officers relate?), it's okay—I prefer the back row, too. And yes, we can't watch an episode of C.O.P.S and loudly sing: "Bad boys, bad boys." And even though I can't have a conversation with a new person without assuming they're guilty until proven innocent (thanks to the cop's daughter in me), I still love you. I've walked away with a few cop tricks up my sleeve anyway and can now speak fluently in police lingo and ten-codes, so that's a plus. Besides, I still feel quite confident that I could name-drop my way out of a speeding ticket. Now that you're almost five years deep into retirement, the worst I have to deal with these days is constant FaceTime calls and weekly lunch dates with you because you're a bored retired guy. But that's not so bad, I know your granddaughter sure appreciates all of the time she can get with her grandpa.

Dad, you were an exceptional police officer and the force is poorer without you. You're a superb father, a strong husband and the best grandpa in the entire world. We may have endured a rocky road or two but the feeling of having you back full-time, knowing that you're safe and sound at home, is priceless. You're a hero to so many but especially to me.

For those reading this, take it all for what you will. If you are the daughter, son, wife, loved one, or close friend of an active or retired police officer, firefighter, or first responder, especially one who is battling or has battled PTSD, then I encourage you to choose grace. Never give up on them. They've walked through hell and back. Even if it feels like you're walking that fiery road with them, keep marching and never let go of their hand.

Thank you to my dad and all our men and women in uniform for your extraordinary acts of service. I will always back the blue.

I don't feel deserving, but I will graciously and humbly accept every word that my daughter Amanda and son Danny put together. I know they put up with a lot before and after I retired, especially when I distanced myself from them. I cannot undo any damage that I may have caused but I can make every day forward count positively. I'm genuinely grateful that they hung in there with me and that they now understand a little bit more about PTSD and their dad. I will never let another day go by where I ever miss anything of importance in their lives again. I know they have my back until the day I die and I have theirs.

CHAPTER 12

The Perspective of a Police Officer's Wife

THIS CHAPTER IS my wife Brenda's perspective, who, thankfully, said yes to marry me in the year 1986. You are my life and my best friend. I will spend the rest of my life ensuring your happiness.

Over to her . . .

I remember the day my husband, Steve, told me he was going to be a police officer. We were in Oklahoma, visiting our family. One of the family members was Steve's cousin, who worked as a police officer in a neighboring city.

During that visit, Steve did a ride-along with his cousin while on duty. After that ride along, Steve did not express much, but I knew in my heart that something in him had changed.

After being home for about a week, I was packing and preparing to move into our new home. While we both were packing boxes, out of nowhere, Steve told me he was going to become a cop.

He told me that he felt it was his calling to help others. I will never forget that day.

There is one thing that I know for sure, and that is when Steve says he is going to do something, he does it! He's a man of his commitment.

Shortly after that, he made plans and went to the police academy at night and continued to work during the day.

His time at the police academy was a fun time for us because our children and I acted out bad guys. I cannot tell you how many times Steve played scenarios out with us and took us into custody. Our children and I wore handcuffs pretty much every week during his training. Those were great memories, and we still laugh at them today. Once Steve graduated from the academy, he left his very high-paying job to go to a very low-paying job. He first became a reserve officer and then took on an additional paid job as a dispatcher; both jobs were with the same department. Those two jobs motivated him even more to pursue his goal of becoming a full-time cop. Steve has always worked multiple jobs to make sure he fulfilled all our needs.

The first time he took a test for becoming a full-time police officer, he couldn't get it. I was still so proud of him because he was not upset, he told me that it was not his time, but next time it would be.

He continued studying and physically training harder than ever, which eventually paid off.

In November 1998, I got a call from him. He was recruited as a police officer. He was so proud that he was in tears. I was proud, too, because he had worked so hard and, throughout the process, some people did not think he would follow through. There was never a doubt in my mind.

From start to finish, law enforcement was a part of our lives for approximately twenty years. The police department that Steve worked for, was extremely good to us. However, the retirement plan in place at the time was not very good.

I will, however, say that the police job changed him and me forever.

I can say that without a doubt, and I know many would agree. My husband was a remarkable police officer and was loved and respected by almost all the people he caught an eye with. He was loyal to his agency and always had the best of intentions. He genuinely wanted to help everyone and still does.

So much happened during his career that I would have to write an entire book to explain it all. The first five years or so, I worried a lot! I eventually gave this worry to God and prayed, prayed, and prayed. I prayed every day, and the Lord was faithful and protected my husband. Steve rarely lost his path, but when he did, he always fought back harder to stay on track. He struggled with his faith but never gave up on that, thank you God! Life was not perfect, and we had a couple of major relationship issues. He came home twice during our marriage and told me that he had sold our house and we were moving. He was a bit selfish at times, but I knew he was trying to improve our financial situation. I did not allow him to do that a third time. Concerning the major relationship issues we had, most couples wouldn't even have made it through, but we always managed to work through them and never gave up on each other.

Towards the end of his career, I started to see a major change in him. I felt that he could no longer shut things off from the calls he had taken and couldn't manage to leave them at work. He began talking about his calls, which he never really did before unless they were funny. The first bad call I remember him talking and crying about was when he went to a suicide call that involved a young girl whom he knew personally. This young girl had hung herself from her closet hanger rod. He said he did a CPR(Cardiopulmonary resuscitation) on her for several minutes while her mother kneeled beside him, crying hysterically and begging him to save her daughter's life. Unfortunately, the young girl died that night. That was the call that made me start to notice a sad change in Steve. He began talking more about calls, which was something new because Steve had typically kept us sheltered from the bad things.

His sleeping started to suffer, which was bad anyway due to all the hours he put in at work. He barely slept, and when he did, it was restless. There were times when he would fight in his sleep or get up from the bed and knock things off the dressers and break lamps. One time, he sat up in bed, screaming, then jumped on top of me as if he was going to punch me. My loud screaming got his attention, and he laid back down, caught his breath, and went back to sleep. He did not remember these episodes, but, trust me, I do.

If Steve asked me to wake him up at a certain time, I would have to touch his feet with a broomstick and speak quietly because if I woke him up any other way, he would wake up swinging.

He also became reclusive and did not enjoy the things he used to. When he was home, he was quiet, angry, and did not want to do anything with people, which was a big red flag because he was usually highly active and loved being around others. He also stopped attending family functions. There were several times I had to make excuses to explain why he was not there, knowing that he was at home just sitting in front of the television. This was a tough one because Steve had become unapproachable and would get incredibly angry if I pointed out his faults.

I saw this change in him, and so did his family, close friends, and his daughter and son.

I began to pray harder than ever before. I did not know what else to do.

I believe the next thing that happened came about through prayer, and I'm forever grateful for it. Our daughter and son began to let Steve know their true feelings about him and how they missed him and wanted him back in their lives. They were becoming frustrated and got increasingly blunt with him as time passed. Then, our daughter sent a text message to him while he was on patrol, asking him to retire.

That day, he came home from work and told me he was retiring. He was tired and wanted his family back. He said he wanted to be the person he was before being a cop. I had no idea at that time how hard that was going to be for him. I will never forget that day, either.

Two weeks later, his career came to an end.

Steve had owned several businesses throughout his law enforcement career and had also obtained his real estate license and became the owner of our own travel business. He was now depending on real estate and our travel business to pay the bills. When he retired, he had zero real estate deals. Our travel business was not growing either, because he did not want to talk with anyone. To be honest, he did nothing but sit around for the first couple of months after his retirement.

I had no idea that things would still be hard after his retirement. The first two to three years were the hardest. He had horrible mood swings and a major identity crisis.

He could not watch the news because if something terrible happened, he felt like he was not doing his part.

He had a major meltdown one day inside of a Lowe's store, which got both our attention and made him think that he may have PTSD. However, his pride would not allow him to address that. It took him years to get help with it; I wish he would have listened to me sooner.

After the Lowe's meltdown was the first time that he ever really talked to me about how he was feeling and what had happened to him in the store, I learned a lot that day and began my own study on PTSD. That helped me to understand more about what he was going through, like being angry, sad, and not talking for several days, as well as fitting with his earlier explanations of his PTSD episodes. I began to understand him more and more each day and started to learn the signs in his behavior and posture when an episode was about to kick off. I learned how to react.

I would highly recommend that all spouses who are married to active or retired police officers consider getting professional help, too. I found there is nothing wrong with getting help and talking to someone, whether it be a friend, someone at church, or another family member or friend, who has been through this type of situation.

I watched my husband fight daily in an attempt to get back to being the person he was before becoming a cop. His PTSD episodes still appear to this day, and he still cannot watch the news, but he can work through them quickly now instead of taking a week or so to get over them. His strength amazes me.

Steve started getting better when he put his pride aside; those are his words, not mine, but I agree.

He began talking to me more about his thoughts and how he felt and began asking me how I felt, too. He started thinking about my feelings. At the beginning of his retirement, I was afraid to ask him questions or ask him anything. I just didn't want to bring up any bad memories, but I found that the more we talked about it, the better we both became.

When Steve finally decided to talk to a counselor, I was relieved, because he realized that he wasn't being weak or any less of a man by facing his issues. When his episodes happened, he would get furious at himself because he felt embarrassed. Finding out that he wasn't crazy, which he learned from the counselor, changed his life.

Throughout all this, I learned things about my husband that I didn't previously know, some of those things hurt me and made me angry, while others were just plain frightening. We discussed the negative choices he had made in his life, for instance, his addictions. But most alarming to me were his thoughts of suicide and the anger he held within him. How did I not know these things? That's why I always say not to be afraid to ask questions.

Steve's law enforcement changed our lives forever, but we both agree that it was part of our journey together to get to where we are in life today—at peace.

We only pray that our story may have some positive effect on other people going through similar challenges.

Steve accomplished his goal, which was and still is putting other people first, and that has made it all worth it.

I am proud of my husband and his accomplishments and everything we have accomplished together. We are a strong and unified force. I am thankful he has taken steps to get the help he needed to feel better. I am grateful for all the people in our lives.

I am most thankful that Steve is more of a godly man than ever. Thank you, God. I am thankful that Steve and I stayed together through it all. Steve and I have been married since 1986, and I love him more than ever, and we are in this life together forever.

I had no idea how Steve's law enforcement career would mold him or how it would change our lives, but it did. Some of it has been good, some bad, but I have come to realize that the police job will be a part of our lives forever. The journey has been a roller coaster ride but worth holding on to.

Steve and I call ourselves survivors of the job. I'm proud of all the police officers and their families out there in this crazy but beautiful world. I pray for you all every day.

CHAPTER 13

Ricki and Ricky

M Y WIFE BRENDA and I first met this wonderful man, and his beautiful bride, several years ago on our first cruise through our travel business. We were sitting at a dinner table together on the first night of the cruise. They introduced themselves as Ricki and Ricky, and the first thing I observed about them was their bubbly personalities. It also did not take us long to figure out how much in love they were with each other.

I was still a cop at the time and was a bit standoffish. Honestly, I was a bit angry about them sitting next to us because that forced me to have to speak.

While speaking to them throughout dinner, we found that we had a lot in common. We both had owned our own business with the same travel company. Mr. Ricky was a retired cop from New York. We shared a friendship with one of my dispatchers. We had both been married to the same person for a long time. We all lived in Colorado—and the list went on.

We pretty much spent the entire week with Ricki and Ricky and shared some fantastic times. One of the funniest times was when we were sitting in the pool together, and Mr. Ricky remembered that his phone was still in his pocket. Not funny at the time, but we laugh about it now.

After that cruise, I told my wife that Ricki and Ricky were brought into our lives for a reason, not knowing why until recently. Ricki and Ricky have been a fantastic influence in our lives. They are the most positive people we know, and they demonstrate love and compassion. When we attend events together, people surround them; and not just because of Mrs. Ricki's homemade cookies, but that they simply bring joy!

When I explained the purpose of this book and asked them to be a part of it by bringing their perspectives on being a retired first responder family, they did not hesitate. Mr. Ricky and I spent some time talking and learned a bit more about one another. Their lack of hesitation led to taking our friendship to a whole new level.

I have the utmost respect for them, and I'm grateful to them for sharing their story. So, enjoy! Here is what Mr. Ricky had to say:

My name is Richard L. Arroyo, Jr. I am a Retired NYPD Detective.

From day one in the NYPD Academy, we were taught to never take what happened on the job personally. I have always been the kind of person who looks at the glass as half-full. My dad, uncle, and cousin were all police officers in NYPD and Nassau County PD when I got on the job.

I watched my dad take the job very personally. So, for me, I knew that my life on the job would be very different. I decided to separate my work life from my home life. My wife never really knew what I did. There were times that I would tell her funny things that happened, but never the things that I saw or did at work.

When I was home, I was her husband, her friend, and Daddy to our children. If I got injured at work, I would always call her from the hospital, so that she could hear my voice and know that I was okay. This was before cell phones.

Since I was a teenager, I always held that when something happens to you, your mindset would determine how you handled the challenge.

My final line-of-duty injury was what caused me to retire on disability. I just want to tell you about two separate incidents that took place at the end of my career.

The first was my final injury, which caused me to leave the job. The second one took place while I was out sick waiting for the board to approve my line-of-duty injury so that I would receive a disability pension.

While I was working in Brooklyn Central Robbery, I had left my office to get something to eat for lunch. While I was driving down the street by myself (high crime areas require that you always work with a partner in an A House), I spotted one of the suspects from one of my cases. I pulled the car over ahead of where he was. As he approached me, I exited my vehicle and confronted him on this very crowded Brooklyn street. As we were talking, a crowd began to gather. I informed him that I was placing him under arrest. At this point, the crowd began to egg him on.

This is where he and I had a real difference of opinion as to what was going to happen next. He thought that it was in his best interests not to cooperate with me and decided that he was going to stab me instead. As you can imagine, this idea did not coincide with my plans. So, the battle began. I had no time to call for backup and the locals were not going to do it for me. We wound up on the ground, with me essentially fighting with one hand, while the other hand was keeping the knife at bay. I was finally able to grab my Motorola Radio and strike him on his head, causing the blood to flow down his face. This made him drop the knife and hold his head with both hands. I immediately flipped him on to his stomach, grabbed his arms, and cuffed him. I then lifted him up and got him in the car before the crowd got violent.

As you can imagine, my adrenaline was pumping pretty well by this time. I took my prisoner to the hospital, and he was treated and released in my custody. Now it was back to my precinct to process the arrest.

I mentioned my adrenaline before because this played an important part in my injury. I bet that you're wondering how that is possible. Let me tell you. It took my body about two days for my adrenaline levels to return to normal. It was around that time that I finally realized I was injured. As I told you, after I had cuffed him, I lifted him up (dead weight) and put him in the car. When I did that, I herniated three discs in my lower back, which explained the intense pain that I was experiencing.

The second event was as follows:

I had already been out sick with my injury and had filed my papers for disability retirement. Part of being out sick is a visit to the police surgeon. In the NYPD, we have unlimited sick pay. The city is self-insured, so we don't have workman's compensation but receive a normal paycheck. Sounds great, right! Well, here is what actually happens: I was visiting the police surgeon, whose facility is in a high crime precinct with only metered parking. They want to make it inconvenient for you! The police surgeon's sole purpose is to get you back to work, while your sole purpose is to try to get healthy.

So, during the visit, I had to go downstairs to put coins in the meter to avoid getting a ticket. Imagine: it's 3:00 pm and there's *a school across from where I'm parked, and the kids were just getting out. As I put my last coin in the meter, I heard shots fire. Remember, I worked there, so I was familiar with the area. I had a general idea where the shots had come from. I also knew there were four different directions in which they could go; one of those directions was where I was standing. Well, the shooter chose the three directions that included me. I saw people running and screaming. It was then that I saw the suspect turn down the street heading towards me, the gun in his hand. I took cover behind a car (I had my gun and shield, no cuffs, no vest, and no additional ammo). I knew he was carrying a semi-automatic pistol, but what I didn't know was its caliber or how many rounds he had left in his magazine. I had only a .38 caliber revolver with five rounds.*

As the shooter approached me, I stood up and confronted him, identifying myself as a police officer. I repeatedly told him to drop his weapon. He was starting to slightly raise the hand holding the gun. I was slowly starting to squeeze my trigger. Our eyes locked—and he put the gun on the ground!

Why did I tell you about these two incidents? Because in both cases, they happened accidentally. You never know what can happen! Both times, things could have gone differently very quickly. Both times God protected me and kept me safe.

Please don't judge an officer for shooting somebody. They have a split second to decide whether to shoot. If he had raised his hand just a fraction more, I would have had no choice but to shoot him.

I had a wife and children waiting at home for me, and that's where I intended to go! I worked my entire career mostly in high crime areas. I was extremely active and made a lot of arrests.

In my final years, I noticed a pattern. I was getting injured more frequently. So, when I was injured the last time, I knew that it was time for me to retire. The odds were beginning to change, and they were not in my favor!

I also noticed that part of my personality had changed, and not in a good way. So, on December 31, 1990, I officially retired. In hindsight, I realized that it took five years following retirement before I got back to the person I was before I got on the job.

While I was on the job, and after I retired, I watched my father become an alcoholic. The job had changed him in a negative way. His perspective towards the changes that were taking place on the job was negative. He took things personally, made poor decisions, and caused disharmony at home with my mother and my sisters. He would get drunk and say hurtful things to them. He refused to get help. His destructive behavior caused his body to suffer through his drinking and his pent-up anger.

There was no talking to him about his problems. We went from having a very close relationship to having no relationship at all. Everything was about his perspective. It was always a 'poor me' attitude. It was never about the choices he had made. He took no responsibility for his words or actions.

In 2005, fifteen years after my retirement, my wife started her first business. Sometime that year, she came to me and said she was worried about me. She said she thought I was changing and becoming withdrawn. My wife is my ride or die. She is my best friend. So, we sought out a therapist and I started taking counseling.

After a few years, we felt that I was in a good place. In 2010, we joined a travel club and became representatives. In 2011, we attended a training course for the travel club. The trainer put on skits to teach us how to do the business. After viewing one of his skits, I found myself crying uncontrollably, and I was the only one in my area to react that way. My wife and I knew that something was wrong but were unaware of what it could be. So, the following week it was back to the therapist (twenty-one years after my retirement). I explained what had happened to me and what the skit was about; it was quickly determined that I was suffering from PTSD. It turns out I had survivor's guilt! The therapist suggested doing EMDR as part of my counseling.

Eye movement desensitization and reprocessing (EMDR) is a form of psychotherapy developed by Francine Shapiro in the 1990s, where the person being treated is asked to recall distressing images; after which the therapist directs the patient in one type of bilateral sensory input, such as side-to-side eye movements or hand tapping. It is included in several evidence-based guidelines for the treatment of post-traumatic stress disorder (PTSD).

The 2013 World Health Organization practice guideline says, 'Like cognitive behavioral therapy (CBT) with a trauma focus, EMDR aims to reduce subjective distress and strengthen adaptive beliefs related to the traumatic event.[18]

Unlike CBT with a trauma focus, EMDR does not involve (a) detailed descriptions of the event; (b) direct challenging of beliefs; (c) extended exposure; or (d) homework.

We worked on this until I was in a good place. People close to me know that I am not super-religious. I do strongly believe in God, though. I had come to terms with the fact that God must have had other plans for me, and it was not my time to go.

I was involved in a lot of severe situations during my time on the job, situations that could have gone bad very quickly. When

---

[18] Guidelines for the management of conditions specifically related to stress. Geneva, Switzerland: World Health Organization; 2013

I look back, it was God who kept me safe. You may or may not believe in God, but I know that if it weren't for God, I would not be here now!

I was raised to believe that men don't cry or talk about their feelings. I must tell you that I do both, and I am not ashamed of it!

If you need help, please go and get it! We have a saying in the NYPD, 'It's better to be judged by twelve than carried by six!' I don't care how tough you are or how macho you think you are. When you need professional help, go and get it.

Respect yourself enough to help yourself. Back in my time on the job, if you asked for help, you were looked at as being weak. If you went to the department psychologist, your career was over. Thank goodness things have changed for the better.

I want you to understand that I truly LOVED my job. I had a great career both in uniform and in plain clothes. I went to units where I wanted to work, and to the schools I wanted to attend, including the FBI National Academy.

When I retired, people would ask me if I missed the job. My answer was always the same—NO! I missed some of the people I worked with, with whom I am still in touch to this day.

On December 31, 2020, I will be retired for thirty years. With God's help, I hope I will be around for another thirty years.

Please know that I am not an expert; I am just a regular person like you. I have always known that it is ten percent of what happens to you and ninety percent of what you do with it.

May God bless you and keep you safe!

Don't be afraid to ask for help! You have spent your entire career responding to calls where people were asking for help. WHY NOT YOU?"

Now, here's what Mrs. Ricki had to say:

"Hi, I'm Ricki Arroyo, wife of Richard (Ricky) L. Arroyo, Jr. Life as a police officer's wife is very different from the regular nine to five, Monday to Friday life.

Ricky went on the job four months after we got married. He was in the New York City police academy for six months. He was then assigned to the twenty-fourth precinct in Harlem. When he made an arrest, he wouldn't get home for three days. Ricky worked around the clock. He worked weekends and holidays. I was working nine to five, Monday to Friday, in the garment industry in NYC. Tough for newlyweds!

Ricky never brought the job home with him. Only the funny stories.

We went to parties with our friends, other police families, and couples. The wives would talk about what happened on the job. I knew NOTHING. I felt so STUPID. I know Ricky was protecting me, and I'm grateful for that, but I still felt STUPID.

I was a mother to our three daughters, all two years apart in age. So, my days were filled. When Ricky closed his locker at the precinct, he left the job there. He walked in our door, and he was Daddy and my husband. Honestly, it made our life as calm and peaceful as it could be. Holidays and weekends were lonely. We would be with family on the holidays, but Ricky's absence caused a huge void.

There were times when I would get a phone call at 4 a.m. from Ricky:

'Hi Hon, what are you doing?'

I'd say: 'I'm sleeping.'

He'd continue, 'I'm good! I'm in the hospital. As soon as they check me out, I'll be heading home. I love you!'

'I love you too!' I'd say.

When Ricky was home on sick leave for two weeks, the girls and I loved him being home. No worries, no stress.

Ricky says that I raised our daughters because I was a stay-at-home mom. That was our choice back in the seventies and eighties. It worked for us. Ricky never had to worry about our girls because I was always home. It was my sole responsibility to take care of our daughters, our dogs, and our home.

Earlier I mentioned how Ricky had told me that he thought his personality was changing, and not in a good way. He had to shut off some of his emotions to survive the job. Yes, it changed him; but, thankfully, he came back to himself five years after he retired.

Yet, in 2005, fifteen years after his retirement, I got worried about Ricky again. He was withdrawn. I thought he was depressed. We're partners in this life and best friends. When one person shuts down, it can kill the relationship. Communication is key! I'm grateful that Ricky listens to me and hears me. He took action. We found out he had PTSD centered around survivor's guilt. Our therapist did EMDR with Ricky a few times, which helped tremendously.

Thank God, I didn't know what happened on the job. I would've never slept, and been anxious and worried all the time.

One thing I admire about my husband is his compassion. It's one of the reasons I fell in love with him. When something happens and affects him deeply, he'll cry. Crying is a natural response and a human feeling. It's like a pressure cooker; you have to let off steam. Crying is a release and is healthy.

The life expectancy of an NYPD officer after retirement is only five years! I'm so grateful that Ricky's coming up on thirty years retired. Thank you, God!

I'm so proud of Ricky. He enjoyed the job and made it work for him. He took advantage of the opportunities the job offered, such as studying at different schools and the FBI National Academy. To be accepted into the FBI NA, you must be at a high level in your police department, such as sergeant, lieutenant, captain, chief, etc. But Ricky was accepted as a police officer.

My husband is the greatest man I've ever known. He's not perfect and neither am I. But we are always willing to learn from each other and grow together.

God bless all of you; and please, stay safe. Please take care of yourselves, your families, and your relationships.

Remember, communication is key.

CHAPTER 14

The MacGyver Perspective

HERE IS A perspective from one of the most brilliant men I know, and I'm proud to say that we are related.

People have referenced him as MacGyver. For those who don't know of MacGyver, let me explain. MacGyver was an ABC TV series that aired from 1985 to 1992. If you search the internet for TV shows during this period, you'll find a description of the program that states the following: 'Angus MacGyver is a secret agent who refuses to carry a gun with him, but fortunately never needs one. Drawing on a vast practical knowledge of science, MacGyver can make use of anything around him to create solutions to any problem he faces.' This description describes the next writer to a tee. If it's broken, he can fix it, and if he needs something, he will build it before he buys it. Also, he is blessed with a good heart, does charity, and helps others.

Here's what he had to say when I asked him to write his perspective after retiring as a first responder.

My name is Tracy Haze, and I am Steve's brother-in-law. I spent just short of thirty-five years working for a municipal fire department. The department I worked for serves the city that

I was born and raised in and still call my home. During my career, we grew from a small city with four fire stations and about forty-five line firefighters serving a community of almost one hundred and fifty thousand residents to six fire stations, and over one hundred and fifty commissioned firefighters. I spent five years as a firefighter/EMT, sixteen years as an engineer, and the last thirteen years as a lieutenant. I loved being part of the ground crew and had no interest in being promoted to a position where I was not posted on the front line.

I was raised in a family of metropolitan police officers, and service was ingrained into me from an early age. Among my police officer relatives, there was an assortment of attitudes toward the career. One uncle rode the fast track to the top and had a very positive attitude about the job. To this day, he appears to maintain a positive outlook on life and is enjoying his retirement. Another uncle was involved in an officer-involved shooting incident early in his career and had acted in defense of a fellow officer. He had a very sour attitude towards the job and had told me he 'would kick my butt if I became a police officer.' He did not exhibit any outward signs of the stress that he carried, such as substance abuse or family issues, but he retired as early as he could and did not live long past his retirement.

When I became a firefighter, I could not imagine the things I would see or be exposed to over my career. As first responders, we have a front-row seat to the greatest show on earth. Each one of us has stories that the layperson would find unbelievable even though in the retelling of those stories, we could never fully convey the derangement of the human spirit that we often witnessed. In other words, what we saw is so much worse than what we could describe.

As a firefighter, I had the benefit of having my fellow crew members around me when we experienced those traumatic events. As a group, we could talk it out to help process what we had been a part of. This is a real luxury compared to our police brothers and sisters, who were often alone in their patrol units and did not have anyone to debrief with. Anyone from the outside who eavesdropped on our conversations would have found most of them to be very distasteful. From the outside, 'blue humor' is most often misunderstood as being boastful or vulgar and not looked at as the coping mechanism that it really is.

"From the beginning of my career through my retirement, and even now, my primary sounding board has been my wife. During our evening telephone calls or on days off following shifts in which we had seen some particularly disturbing scenes, I could talk through the scenes with her without being judged. It seemed that by talking about it, I was able to process and filed away the often-graphic things that we had to deal with. Midway through my career, my wife observed that I could never recall the names of the people I had treated or helped. During *emergency scenes, I made it a point to speak on a personal level with my patients. I referred to them by name and even documented those names on subsequent reports. But, after the call was over, I could barely remember the names I had just used in my conversations with them. My wife and I concluded that this was my mind's way of remaining at arm's length from the situations that I was involved in. This was good because I was worried that I might be exhibiting the initial symptoms of some form of name-related dementia.*

I consider myself fortunate to have been able to separate myself from most of the often-graphic events that I was part of. I could tell you about the unbelievable depravity that some people exhibit, the creative ways, and the great lengths some people go to while making a statement about attempting to end their life or the loss of the lives of loved ones. I cannot describe the sadness of watching new parents grieve over the loss of a baby or of a spouse bidding goodbye to their lifelong companion. I have repeatedly witnessed the incomprehensible attraction of an addict towards their substance of choice. I have held the hands of people as they passed from this world into the next, and I have prayed for many souls, not entirely sure where they would end up. To temper the bad things I have seen, I can say that I have been part of sixteen childbirths in the field and have witnessed more lives being saved than I can count.

First responders are often in need of help. Some know it, but most don't, and they would never call 911 to get that help. It is a good thing that crisis intervention teams, post-incident stress debriefings, department psychologists, peer support, and EAP programs have been developed and introduced for the first responders. It's disturbing to note that it is only in the last decade that it has become socially acceptable to use these services in the firehouse or police station setting.

In my department, we had numerous individuals who ended up as alcoholics, and as a result had failed marriages or careers. Others internalized their feelings to the point where they could not function in the basic aspects of life, much less make split-second critical decisions or actions on the job. Most of these people worked with close-knit crews, who knew the underlying issue but were not personally equipped to deal with it or aware about the available resources that would help their friends and coworkers. Each of us responds differently to the stress of the job, and we all process things our way. Some of my coworkers could open up in a group post-incident debriefing, while others felt more comfortable talking one-on-one with a peer counselor. I could not do either. If I could not sort my feelings out by critiquing the call with my crew, I would talk it over with my wife. On the occasions when that didn't help, I felt myself clam up and would end up processing the feelings in my head. This often resulted in lost sleep, a lack of appetite, no energy in the gym, distraction, and other unhealthy symptoms.

One of the deputy chiefs of my fire department had a career-long interest in health and wellness. He was ahead of his time, as this has now gained an equal footing with mental health in the fire service. Over the years, this chief arranged for us to receive all sorts of medical and fitness testing from some of the most highly recognized experts. Our crews were often the subjects in evaluations that were later used to develop health guidelines that are now used in the fire service nationwide. This chief was a friend, and it was through him that my interest in the relationship between our jobs and our physical health began. As I studied this relationship, I learned that our physical health and mental wellbeing are inter-related.

One of the primary things that I discovered about the health of first responders is that they are all sleep-deprived, which seems pretty obvious, isn't it? A person needs to progress through the various levels of sleep to get to the deeper levels where our bodies repair themselves both physically and mentally. We work out in the gym to build our bodies and make them stronger. But, if we don't get to the third level of non-REM sleep, our bodies do not produce the hormones necessary to repair the tissues that we break down when we work out. The third level also helps us in maintaining a strong immune system. We also need to reach the fourth level of sleep or the REM phase, for our mind to process the emotions that we experience during the day and to file away what we have learned. Without reaching these later stages of sleep, we cannot repair our bodies or our minds.

A lot has been said about the importance of counseling in processing the emotions that we encounter as part of our job serving our communities. There is also a physical aspect that must be addressed if we want to help our fellow first responders process the unthinkable things which they encounter on the job. The police officers work shifts that do not play well with the demands of family life. The firefighters are rudely woken up several times each night while on the shift. A police officer friend of mine loves to work the graveyard shift. He also takes on day-time extra duty assignments, such as providing security at the local businesses that contract with the PD for their services. Most firefighters I know have second jobs or side businesses to help make ends meet. Sleep is usually sacrificed to accommodate the rest of the demands on their schedules. Depression, irritability, an inability to concentrate or make decisions, and weight gain are all signs of a lack of sleep. How many of you know someone who demonstrates these traits?

I have always been a believer in Jesus Christ. About fifteen years ago, my fire department created a Fire Department Chaplain position and brought on an ironworker with a Ph.D. in theology. We had an instant connection, and I can credit him with much of the sanity that I maintained in the later part of my career. He would visit the stations, and I often felt bad that he and I would talk the entire time that he spent at my station. When we had calls during his visits, I had him ride along with me so that we could continue our conversations. Growing up and attending church weekly during my youth had given me a very superficial understanding of Christianity. It was this man who taught me how to apply the Bible to my daily life. It helped me understand that God did not put me in my situation so that I could dwell on what other people did. He put me there so I could help as many of them as I could. I began talking in-depth with my patients about the circumstances in their lives. I began to find peace with the bad things I saw that I could not control because I knew I was not in control. It helped me to accept the things that happened around me without questioning them.

Looking back, I feel blessed to have survived a long career in the fire service. I feel fortunate to have stumbled through the early part without any real trauma (mental or physical) as I wasn't equipped to deal with it back then. I am thankful to have had the support systems around me in the form of family and friends to help me process the things when the events began to pile up later on. Late in my career, I realized that there are many options available to help first responders deal with the things they see and to maintain at least a minimal level of faith in humanity. Just like the strategy and tactics that we use to control any emergency scene, our ability to cope with these insults takes a multi-pronged approach. If you find yourself nearing your breaking point, please try to address all the things that will help you get better. Talk to someone you trust, whatever form that takes, maintain your physical health, get lots of sleep, and, if you haven't yet, get to know God.

Tracy's wife, who is also my sister Kathy, will be sharing her perspective next on her life while being married to a first responder. She has put a positive spin on her perspective, and that's because of her protective nature, her loving and positive attitude, and her unwavering support of her husband. However, I do know that there has been a road bump or two but despite that my sister and brother-in-law have persevered through. All I have to say about that is I'm proud of both of them.

Kathy and my other sister Connie, whom you read about earlier, are two of my most trusted people in the world. They have had a great deal to do with my success and gave me the motivation to keep progressing forward. They have amazing strength and are committed to improving the lives of others. I'm honored to have these sisters on my side.

So, here's what Mrs. Kathy Haze had to say:

Being the wife of a firefighter is not for the faint of heart. Tracy and I have been married for thirty-four years. A couple of days after we were married, he was hired onto our city's fire department. This ride has shaped our marriage, the adolescence of our two daughters, the people who we've grown to be over the last three decades, and the life we are making together in retirement.

The role of a firefighter's wife is both rewarding and challenging. Over the last thirty-four years, our family has adjusted to meet the needs of the fire department schedule that often encroaches on holidays and special events. Our two daughters, who grew up with Tracy working in the department, knew that if he worked Christmas day, their presents arrived at least a day early. Holiday gatherings were celebrated days before (or after) the actual holiday. Birthdays and anniversary celebrations were postponed but never forgotten. Thankfully, the majority of Tracy's career was spent working twenty-four hours on and twenty-four hours off, so we were able to spend a large amount of time together. It allowed us to manage a schedule that worked for our girls so that someone was always home. Sports and school events were attended, and our weekends were often spent building memories.

Although he was home two-thirds of the month, it was inevitable that whenever something would happen, he was on shift. Our daughters never needed stitches and rarely got sick when Tracy was on duty. Our house never filled with smoke and the furnace pilot light knew better than to blow out while he was home. Thankfully, Tracy taught me some skills that allowed me to solve such problems when they were mine to fix. For eleven years, he worked at the station that would have also dispatched to our house. That brought a sense of comfort; should something happen bad enough to warrant a call to 911, I knew I would be welcomed with the only face that could make the situation better.

For the better part of the first twenty years that Tracy was in the department, I was able to spend that time with our daughters. On the days he was on shift, our girls and I made memories and developed a bond unattainable without such circumstances. As hard as it was wearing every hat while he was on shift, I would never trade those memories and the bond that has lasted well into adulthood. When he was hired on, a fellow fire wife shared with me that you get used to your alone time and begin to look forward to it. I found an appreciation of time to myself, but Tracy is my best friend, and being without him was difficult. When our daughters grew up and created separate lives of their own, I spent a lot more time by myself. During these times, I ate dinners alone, went to church by myself, and knew I had only myself to depend on. At the end of Tracy's career, the department chose to switch the schedule to forty-eight hours on and ninety-six hours off, which meant that I was without him for two continuous days. Even after being married for thirty-plus years, I still missed him while he was working and anxiously awaited him walking through the door. In the time I was without our girls, I chose to spend it with the Lord. It was during this time that I felt my relationship with Him deepened and I believe that Tracy's retirement is a testimony to God's faithful Word of protection.

It's not to say that because I spent lots of time with the Lord, I didn't worry. I spent one-third of our marriage in a state of constant concern. The anxiety about Tracy being hurt or infected while helping others lingered on my mind with every phone call that ended in "Gotta go!" Some mornings, Tracy would return home, and it was apparent that he'd had a rough shift. But he would insist that he didn't need to talk about it, reassuring me that everything was okay. But on several other occasions, he needed to unload the happenings of the last twenty-four hours. Some calls will forever remain etched in his (and my) mind. There were people that he had to save, words he wished he never had to speak, and things he saw that he can never un-see. But alongside these horrific events, there are also babies he assisted in bringing earth-side, families that are complete because of his and his crew's vigilant efforts, and the world is an overall better place because of the dedication of Tracy and his fellow officers. I thank God every day for watching over my husband while he performed his duty while serving in the department.

Tracy saw some of the most gruesome scenes; he helped people back together, rushed to car accidents where the car no longer resembled its original form, and rescued people from burning buildings. But ask him to pull his daughter's tooth or give an IV to someone he loves and he'll break out into a cold sweat. He could walk into a situation and see images even Hollywood couldn't compete with but crumbles when he sees his girls cry. However, there were parts that he kept guarded, which I can only assume is like so many others in this line of work. He guards himself with an often impenetrable exterior. Even though

Tracy has the heart of a teddy bear, he keeps his feelings and emotions well-guarded. Sometimes, he readily shared some of those experiences, but others he kept locked away. I knew the only thing I could do was to ensure that he knew I was always available to listen to anything he wanted to share. For someone who does not experience these calls first-hand, it is difficult to understand the process of filing them away. I realized this early on, but it never got easier. I rested some concerns when he started to tell me about the conversations that he would share with the department chaplain. This is a man he still holds in high esteem, and I knew God intentionally placed these two together. Their friendship is an everlasting blessing.

The family you gain from being a part of a fire department is unlike any other job-related family. We experience the same fear of our loved ones not returning home, getting sick, or being hurt. On the holidays our spouses were on shift, we celebrated together at the firehouse with the most delicious food. We would consider ourselves lucky if we got through the entire meal without them being called out. The relationships created during Tracy's career have not been lost since his retirement. In fact, the bonds formed were bound by chapters of experiences written in each other's books. I know Tracy and his crew got through the hard times by coping with situations through conversations that the outside world would consider crude and obscene. However, it is a function of the job that maintains sanity and provides a way to cope through such experiences. Even after retiring, he is still a sounding board to his fellow firefighters and spends time talking and visiting with them regularly.

Tracy did more for the fire department than just serve and protect. He was known as the renaissance man who fixed and repaired anything that needed attention. I know Tracy left a legacy and has been told many times that there is a void without his presence. I am proud of the man he is and the imprint he left in those many years as a firefighter, colleague, and friend. Since retiring, we are finding our new normal. We continue to do things together, traveling to the places we said we always would, and making uninterrupted memories. Even after retiring, Tracy still serves. I believe his purpose in this life is to continue to serve God by helping people with the skills he's been blessed with. Whether it's calming a neighbor's fear when her baby spikes a fever or replacing another's fence, he willingly uses his abilities to calm, provide for, and protect others. It's something that is engrained deep down inside him, and retiring isn't going to take that away. Tracy is a man of God, and I am thankful that He protected him through all the dangers he experienced so that we could live a good life together.

CHAPTER 15

A Police Commander's Perspective

T HIS PERSPECTIVE WAS introduced in chapter five, The Patrol Journey, where we had discussed: what happens after taking calls for service and how first responders usually cope.

My story is about how I managed even though there was not a whole lot of external or internal peer support during my years of service, and how it felt unsafe facing a mental breakdown. It's in the nature of cops to always be in control and to not show weakness, which implied career suicide—or the dreaded "Termination." The town did have a counselor on call who was available to the officers, whom they could call even in private if needed, although it was not highly publicized.

So, I reached out to the agency that I had retired from and spoke with my old chief. He advised me that a lot had changed over the years, and they now had a peer support group program in place that was being run by somebody with whom I was very familiar. My chief permitted me to speak with him to get his perspective on mental health.

This particular commander, who was a sergeant back when I was serving, has been more of a blessing in my career and my life than I could have ever imagined. His main role during my tour was to act as my instructor. His duties included training me on how to stay alive, which he is still doing at the time of writing. But now, he's also training officers and guiding them to stay healthy both physically and mentally.

I have the utmost love and respect for that man and his family. I will be indebted to him for life.

Here is what this active police commander has to say:

> Dangerous. That's what we were told at the academy—everything we would do as law enforcement officers would involve danger. Vehicle stops—Dangerous. Pedestrian contacts—Dangerous. Domestic disturbances—Very Dangerous. Stopping to get a cup of coffee at the local convenience store—well, that could be dangerous, too.

> Well-intentioned academy instructors hoped to instill in us a sense of vigilance. Their aim was to create a mindset that would always keep us safe from physical threats. And it probably did. In a way, the cultivation of this mindset was comforting. Comforting because we could prepare for the threats that we might face. If we learned the skills well enough, trained hard enough, and listened to the experiences of veteran officers with sincerity, we too would survive.

But this was only partly right.

We put so much attention on surviving that we forgot about thriving. Physical survival, without argument, had to be a priority. But strategies for navigating an emotionally complex environment were never discussed. Sure, we occasionally talked about the trauma and personal sacrifices each officer had to endure because of "The Job". These conversations were more farcical than therapeutic, of course. They were done in a "badge of honor, rite of passage" sort of way—divorces, addiction, personal conflict, bad diet, and, even worse, lack of sleep.

"Just part of the job. Comes with the territory. Welcome to the club. You'll be fine."

It's caught up to us now. Or perhaps it's always been with us, and we're just now starting to pay attention. This profession is dangerous. For all the reasons we were told in the academy, it turns out that those physical threats we were frequently warned about weren't the most dangerous aspects.

These days, we can paint a much grimmer picture of the dangers of being employed in law enforcement: post-traumatic stress injuries, suicides, and early, unnatural death by numerous causes. The comfort and control we felt in preparing for all those physical threats are not translating to our management of these issues.

Fortunately, the law enforcement profession worldwide is starting to pay attention to these other hidden and often, neglected dangers. Most are going beyond just doing obligatory critical incident debriefs. Many are beginning to leverage a vast pool of resources to address these dangers. Therapists, psychologists, wellness programing, resilience training, substance abuse, addiction counseling, financial wellness courses, diet, nutrition consultation, and analyzing sleeping patterns. Heck, they even offer free yoga.

These types of strategies aren't new and have been used in other fields for decades with great success. But what is the efficacy of it all for law enforcement? Is it reducing the dangers and addressing the core issues? These strategies are perceived as being soft and this results in a stigma associated with many of these strategies. Hence, law enforcement has been a stubborn, and late adopter. It will likely be years before we realize their real benefits.

For now, organizations are spending money on resources, developing wellness programs, and checking the box. Certainly, this is a movement in the right direction. However, it has been my observation that it isn't enough to just provide the resources. We must also convince the officers to engage actively and willingly. We need to do away with the long-held stigma and begin using these resources not as mere treatment, but also as prevention. We're talking about a big cultural change here. A tall order in a profession that excels at suspicion and whose members despise two things:

1. Change

2. The way things are

However, I'm very hopeful that change is around the corner. I see the culture slowly beginning to shift, and some of these new strategies are now being accepted. A part of the credit belongs to the new generation entering the profession. I'm making some broad generalizations, but these new officers typically have the qualities of being emotionally intelligent and they tend to embrace wellness as a lifestyle. In applicant interviews, I regularly hear them explain the importance they place on the quality of living. They are far better equipped to thrive and will be doing extraordinary things for this profession.

But credit is also due to smart organizations that embrace their members as their most valuable resource. Organizations that genuinely care about their employees and their wellbeing. Organizations that are approaching thriving just as we used to approach surviving. They're accomplishing this by presenting it as a new skill set for the officers to learn. Perhaps, we can call it- Officer 'thrival' training—to coin a term.

I'm convinced that officer 'thrival' training is most effective when presented through a skill-based learning approach, which is both culturally competent and normalized. Here is what it looks like:

Skills-based learning approach: Our academy curriculums are designed to give recruits foundational skills and knowledge that sets them on the proper trajectory for their careers. Most (if not all) of these skills are perishable: shooting, driving, arrest control/defensive tactics, search, and seizure. Many states even require that these topics be treated as mandatory by law. Organizations recognize the perishability of these skills and, therefore, regularly revise them as part of an officer's annual in-service training. Once out of the academy, the officers will revisit these skills again and again throughout their careers. This is a time-tested training paradigm.

We've now begun to incorporate 'thrival' training at the foundational level. We're talking with academy recruits about trauma, its symptoms, and more importantly, its prevention. The recruits get exposed to strategies for coping, cognitive-behavioral theory, and even mindfulness training. Moreover, as in survival skills training, the organizations are now adopting 'thrival' skills as part of their regular in-service curriculums.

Culturally competent: Most organizations have historically offered their members free psychological services. Typically, this took the form of a network of providers that members could access to find a practice that was a 'good fit.' Unfortunately, many officers have had the experience of taking the often-enormous and difficult step to visit a counselor or therapist, only to be disappointed (or worse, disheartened) by the whole experience. Frequently, this is because the network of providers available for officers rarely have firsthand experience with the profession. The well-intentioned therapists and counselors simply don't have a frame of reference to understand and assist these officers with what are unique psychological needs. I've even had officers tell me that they've felt guilt after a therapy session. In an attempt to emotionally process a critical incident, they shared details that they believed may have traumatized the therapist.

For many officers, the decision to seek psychological services took months, sometimes years in the making. Often, that first visit will be the only window of opportunity to convince them that they had made the right decision. Recognizing that, organizations are contracting with practices that specialize in first responder therapy. These practices have taken the time to develop an informed cultural competency and have also cultivated close working relationships with local first responder organizations. They can provide services that not only match the unique needs of individual patients but also the needs of a specific organization.

The power of cultural competency can also be seen in peer support programs. These have been a staple of first responder organizations for several decades. Long enough for us to fully recognize their incredible effectiveness and value. Their effectiveness is not only measured by the endorsements of members who have used them but also through relevant research showing that speaking about issues with a fellow member is often just as effective as a session with a professional therapist.

Normalized: It's considered relatively normal to go to your physician or dentist for a checkup. Your friends or co-workers don't normally interpret these visits as a sign that you're sick. On the contrary, they are typically done preventively to rule out any major illness or disease. Organizations often require their members to participate in regular physical tests as a condition of employment.

But, if you were to mention to a co-worker that you had an appointment with a psychologist, they would likely assume that something was wrong, which is the difference between something being normal (seeing a physician or dentist for a checkup) and something being anomalous (having an appointment with a psychologist). The former being considered preventative and the latter being considered the treatment, which is the stigma that must be overcome with 'thrival' strategies. If we are going to overcome it, we must first normalize it.

This takes us back to a skills-based learning approach (early introduction at the academy level and continuous revisiting of the topics throughout an officer's career). But a change in expectations is also in order. Specifically, establishing expectations that the members willingly participate in preventative psychological care. Mandatory mental health checkup programs, similar to physical checkups, are long overdue in this profession. This practice makes sense, it is in the best interest of officers' well-being, and also normalizes it. If everyone is doing it regularly, then it just isn't that big of a deal when someone really needs to go. Whether its preventatively, or because they need therapy to deal with a psychological issue.

The most potent tool in normalizing 'thrival' training is the testimony of fellow officers. I have witnessed officers give a heartfelt endorsement of strategies and resources they utilized to help them through a traumatic experience or personal struggle. Those endorsements resonate with fellow officers and can instantly shatter long-held biases.

The future of thrival: In the past, our profession has often been criticized for being more reactive than proactive. Admittedly, it can take us a while to get rolling. But once we see a problem, we have a tenacious ability to develop solutions. All the topics presented here deserve far more attention than I have given them. But I know organizations around the world are having *more in-depth conversations about them. Therefore, I have great hope for the future of officer 'thrival' training.*

One of the top priorities of our profession has always been the safety and survival of our members. That priority should never change. But it is ready for an upgrade: One that includes not just survival, but thrival. Some may argue that thriving may not be possible for members of this profession. The constant exposure to toxic people and caustic events simply takes an unhealthy toll on our officers, which clearly has been true for many.

But for others, who have approached it from a different mindset, this profession is a great privilege. One that allows its members to get underneath the thin veneer of society and witness the real human condition. That witnessing requires an open mind, a strong sense of self-awareness, and a highly developed set of skills. Skills not dissimilar from the survival skills that I first learned many years ago at the academy. Only now that the skill set must be broader, with some of the vigilance turned inward.

I am proud of what I have seen in the next generation of law enforcement officers. Their level of sophistication leaves no doubt that they will master this new set of skills. They will learn from our mistakes. They will serve with courage and equanimity. They will be remarkably resilient. And of course—they will thrive.

CHAPTER 16

My Mother's Perspective

HERE IS A word from my teacher, my leader, my foundation, my hero, my mom. When I asked my mom what she thought of my career, this is what she had to say:

> My name is Mary, and I'm Steve's mom. It did not surprise me that Steve chose to be a police officer because of how he always wanted to help people and make a difference in peoples' lives. I enjoyed walking into restaurants with Steve when he was in uniform because it felt like I was the one getting all the attention. Steve attracted a lot of attention when he was dressed in his uniform. I'm partial, but he looked handsome. I avoided thinking and worrying about Steve when he was at work, but, I admit, I slept better when he was off duty.

> I would watch the news every night to make sure Steve wasn't on it, which helped me sleep better the nights he was at work. Steve changed towards the end of his career. He became somewhat sad and anti-social with the family. I worried about his health. As his mother, I wish I had picked up on the fact that he was depressed and experiencing symptoms of PTSD. I missed Steve's

smile. My favorite part of Steve's career was when he retired because I felt one less major worry in my life. It took Steve a while to get back to being his old self after he retired. I watched him fight to transition from a negative, bad-tempered person to a strong Christian, who fell more in love with his family than ever. It appears he no longer takes things for granted and truly enjoys life now. I'm proud of how hard Steve has fought for himself and his family. He is back to being the social butterfly that he was before becoming a police officer and has more of a drive to help people in need and to succeed than ever before. I can't wait to see what Steve does next. Most importantly and selfishly, I am so grateful to God that Steve is still here on this earth to help and take care of me.

What a fantastic journey for all these first responder survivors. We can only pray that their perspectives will add value and help impact the lives and futures of those yet to have experienced the depth as a first responder or a first responder family member.

CHAPTER 17

Your Own Mind Can Get You Through It

IT REQUIRES FAITH, opinion, and experience for your mind to get you through it. Still, it does not mean that you should not seek counseling if you are experiencing any signs of anxiety, depression, PTSD or whatever it may be you are experiencing.

Things my mind helped get me through:

Let's start with my finger counting—It doesn't happen as often, but it does rear its ugly little head once in a while, typically when there's a tense situation, or I'm mad or nervous about something. Fortunately for my wife, the finger counting has almost stopped while we are asleep. When it occurs, I recognize it, and I immediately start clenching my hands together or making fists until it passes.

Next, I can still see those red and blue overhead patrol car lights from working the night shift all those years. However, this, too, has become minimal. If it occurs, I get up, get a drink of water, take some deep breaths, maybe eat something, and then go back to bed. Our room is completely blacked out, as well, as I've discovered that it helps too.

Next, the slideshow projector effect: This one is the worst, but it's improving. When this kicks off, I immediately get angry. I tell my mind that I'm going to stop this from happening. I will replace the slideshow pictures with something good that happened in my life—like pictures of my beautiful granddaughter, fun memories, joyful moments, vacations, positive images of family, my activities, and good times. This had resulted in less recovery time from the effects, which has reduced from multiple days to around thirty minutes or less.

Being startled by something, such as loud noises, traffic accidents, sirens that I hear before seeing, and news stories relating to law enforcement are still some of my biggest psychological triggers.

Next, no sleep: A mentor of mine (Steve Moreland of Success Publishing) explained part of this sleeping problem, and he referred to it as the 3 P's, which is problems, pain, and panic. I added in PTSD, as the 4th P. That's why you stay awake at night: It's because you don't know what to do, or you hate your job, or you don't want to go to work, or you want to fire your bosses because they're jerks, or you can't get a pay raise, or it's lousy retirement, or you have no time or money freedom. What's the next step, where do I start, and who can I trust? These are some of the things you can focus your attention on and try to fix them. Don't make excuses, fix the problems; this will fix the pain and reduce the panic. Get your mind and body healthy.

Also, watch for these eight signs that may indicate that you might need a break or may need to see a professional:

1. Being Physically Sick
2. Poor Concentration
3. Poor Quality of Sleep
4. Low Mood, feeling depressed for no apparent reason
5. Lack of Productivity
6. Disengaged from Life and Pleasurable Activities
7. Anxiety
8. Anger or Irritability

Here are a few personal signs of my own that tell you that you may need a break: Taking small, meaningless things personally and shutting people out for days, typically loved ones, feeling overwhelmed, and always feeling tired or lethargic.

I believe the following is a must:

Working out and daily exercise, including a clean diet, is a must for me. If I miss too many workouts, I can feel myself slipping backward, meaning loss of motivation, becoming reclusive, getting angry, and refusing to socialize. Long story short, it's as if you're starving and you become *hangry*, meaning hungry and angry at the same time. Eat! If you feel these on-sets, I recommend forcing yourself to exercise; try it if you don't believe me. I bet you'll feel better than ever after the workout. Not to mention, exercise gets the creative juices flowing.

Invest in self-development and self-improvement. Stay away from anything negative. Eliminate or try to reduce the drama in your life, and eliminate negative people from your life. Still, pray for them but get their negativity out of your head.

Another must: read more books, maybe start with the Bible, or anything related to your personal and spiritual belief system.

I have personally read several books on personal growth, self-development, and entrepreneurship.

These types of books worked for me because I love growing as a person and enjoy people, business, and making money.

Keep your mind working positively. Eliminate additional negative things, such as depressing social media, the news, and pretty much anything on the television. At least, it works for me.

Again, if the negative people around you are not willing to grow with you, you may have to stop hanging around them. Some of the worst pain you can feel throughout your life may come from the people you love or have helped along the way. It can happen, so be prepared to deal with it, forgive, and move on. I'm not necessarily saying forget about it, but if you cannot get past it, it will eat you alive. You know who these people are, and you know they can suck the energy out of you.

Please get involved in something positive, no matter what it is. For example, go to church, start your own business, or find a hobby. But always surround yourself with honest and genuine people, who share your same interests, goals and are continually positive about life and improving their situation.

Take time for yourself! Remember, in chapter nine, where Brian recommended reading specific scriptures? I re-read those scriptures from my Bible in what I call my most spiritual place in the world and my favorite place to take time for myself; Lake Powell, Utah. I remember spending three days in Lake Powell by myself, just sitting in a parking lot that overlooks the lake. Not only did I re-read the scriptures that Brian recommended, but other things took place in those three days, as well. Some personal, but the main thing that happened was I received a call from my son. During the conversation, my son said he called because he was worried about me and felt the need to call and tell me that he loved me and appreciated everything I have done for him. He also said he wouldn't know what to do without me. I call that call 'God's intervention.' It encouraged me to live and fight for my family. It was there that I became closer to God and felt I discovered my life path and purpose.

Pray and fight for your life in private, and it will shine through in public. God gave us a powerful mind for us to use, use it as God intended, which is to do good things, help others, become leaders, and help others to lead, as well.

CHAPTER 18

The New Life Transformation: What Changed?

ELL, BY GOD's good grace, having survived the first few years after retirement, I'm still on this earth. I call this chapter the New Life Transformation, and throughout my entire life, this has been my most blessed turning point ever. All the years I've been alive, and all the times I've felt that something was missing, I've finally found the answer to that riddle now.

But I had to make some massive changes before that answer finally showed itself. I had to get rid of a lot of ego, pride, stubbornness, doubt, anger, and hate, as well as a whole lot of controlling factors to move forward. Even though I had all those things, I was missing belief and courage—faith in God and courage in myself. I let fear control my life, and I did not even know it. I was covering up my life with all the wrong things.

The answer was that I needed to ask for help, I needed help, and I finally realized it. I couldn't do it on my own.

Number one, and most importantly, I stopped doubting God and the power of prayer. "Ask, and it will be given to you; seek, and you will find; knock, and it will be opened to you. For everyone who asks receives, and the one who seeks finds, and to the one who knocks it will be opened."[19]

I teamed up with some very high-level businesspeople through network marketing and listened to their teaching. These mentors kept telling me to read books, take self-development classes, and invest in my mind by taking leadership and financial courses. Don't just invest money into a business, invest in yourself. They made me realize that self-investment is the best investment you can ever do.

After teaming up with people like this and listening to them and applying their advice, I said to myself, "Damn, what do you know? These folks know what they're talking about." Why did it take me so long to realize it? My answer is that I needed to get my mindset back on the right track and ask for help. I had to become the man that God intended me to be, and I can only tell you that you will know in your soul when that happens. It is an unexplainable transformation. Don't wait as I did. There are people out there who are willing to help you achieve success today.

After doing many of the things that my mentors recommended, I now know more than ever about finances. I understand the difference between assets and liabilities, stocks, retirement plans, investments, and what it takes to become successful—personally and financially. Why do I mention this? Here's why: Let's be honest, isn't a lack of money one of the

---

[19] Mt 7:7-8 ESV

biggest problems in most people's lives? I've heard people say so many times that they just can't sleep because they're so worried about money. I don't love money, but we must have it.

I've become more disciplined, determined, and obedient than ever. I have attended courses regarding self-development, building relationships, and the importance of teamwork.

I've learned how to create a habit tracker, a focus board, a creative values list, visualize my goals, make affirmations, read my Bible daily, and know my destiny, how to get there and find my core purpose in life. I believe that until you truly find your purpose in life, your life will not change for the better.

Write your life out on a paper; I found that if you don't write it down, then it's more than likely that it's not going to happen.

I am grateful for my journey and thankful for God and church. Worship is a weapon you can use to work through anything. I'm also incredibly thankful for the fact that I no longer doubt God or the power of prayer. I now know what my life is about, and it's not about my wants or needs but relationships with other people. It's about focusing on helping others to become the best version of themselves. It's about growing into the person we truly want to be and helping people get what they want. Put their needs first, and trust that your wants and needs will follow.

I now realize how my words and actions have affected people to this day, both in good and bad ways. Positive seeds should be the only seeds to be planted and harvested.

It's important to help other people succeed emotionally and financially but, most importantly, to show them how to invest in themselves and their minds, heart, and soul. I call these things part of the transformation process. Figure out who you want to be and go after it with a vengeance until it happens. Don't let anyone or any obstacles stand in your way. One of my mentors, Matt Morris, said it best: "Don't denounce your success because cowards have an opinion."[20]

After this process, I have come to enjoy life much more. I'm surrounded by amazing, supportive, and positive people. My financial strategy is on track, with new opportunities showing up daily. The future of my network marketing and real estate company is bright. I've published my first book called *Limitless Success*. All that I have achieved is based solely on the support and encouragement of so many loyal friends, mentors, and family members.

Without going through my personal transformation, none of this would've ever been possible.

I no longer wake to an alarm clock. I get to hang out more with my son and daughter, who, by the way, are two of the biggest reasons I wake up every day. I'm so proud of them and more grateful to them than they will ever know. I get to see and play with my granddaughter weekly, and I enjoy every minute of watching her grow up. My wife and I have been able to travel to exotic places I never thought would be possible. I have built relationships with new friends, families, and mentors, and with

---

20 Matt Morris, "You Can't Pay Your Bills With Other Peoples Opinions," September 17, 2016, https://www.mattmorris.com/opinions/.

people, I never really knew existed. None of this would have happened without my fight for a new life transformation.

Don't procrastinate any longer. Average people procrastinate, and that is why they live a mediocre life. If you're okay with average, God bless you. I will still care about you and pray for you, but if you're not okay with average, transform.

Don't sweat failure. Don't be ashamed of the times you've failed, but be proud that you get back into the fight. Keep trying to turn a financial loss into a financial win or a life loss into a life win.

The way I look at it, failures will only make you smarter and stronger. Failure inspires winners, and failure defeats losers. Take your failures and turn them into rallying cries.

The whole time I was chasing the dream of being a millionaire, I should've been chasing a dream of being a leader and teaching others to do the same.

I wish the best for everyone who has the will and determination to never quit and to fight for their lives because it's your life, and you only get one shot at it. As Ben Franklin once said (supposedly, at least), "You have the right to pursue happiness, it's up to you to catch it."[21]

I am so grateful for my journey that led me to where I am today.

---

[21] "Misquotes and Memes: Did Ben Franklin REALLY Say That?," Newswise (Baylor University, July 1, 2015), https://www.newswise.com/articles/misquotes-and-memes-did-ben-franklin-really-say-that.

Final Thoughts: Why Fight?

MY PRAYER IS for each person to uplift their opinion and perception of police officers and first responders and backup their thoughts with facts before being so quick to judge. I know we must be realistic and say there will always be people who just don't get it and will never change. Then again, I'll be happy if I can change the thought process of even a single hateful person to a positive perspective on what first responders do in their respective profession.

Next, if you are a first responder or anyone battling with a mental injury, please find any option other than taking your own life. Grasp on to whatever you possibly can. You will not be doing your loved ones a favor by checking out. It will hurt them more than you would ever know. It leaves the survivors feeling guilt stricken, always asking why, how did I not know, and what could I have done differently?

I know this because I have experienced the act of suicide not only on a professional level, but in my personal life, from wanting and taking a substantial step to end my own life, as well, bear witness to several suicides within my own family. I do not have the answer to this completed result, and I'm pretty sure that there is nothing I can say to make the survivors of suicide feel better, but I will tell you this from my own experience. I know that a suicide attempt is a dark and lonely place to be in. At that potentially final and fatal moment, there are several roller coaster rides of emotions. I never blame anyone for the position I found myself in. I still felt an enormous amount of love for my wife and children, family members, and anyone who treated me kindly. I felt unbearably exhausted; my mind was in a constant spin and filled with sad memories. I felt as if I had no more to offer anyone. I felt as if I could not repent for my sins. The scary thing is, I felt all of this while being stone-cold sober. That's the only way I can explain that moment. I only survived that day because of a split-second intervention. I'm truly sorry for those of us who have lost anyone to suicide. To the survivors, feel no guilt. That's all I have to say about that!

If you have suicidal thoughts, please call anyone and reach out to them, it's okay, trust me, they will understand and be more than happy to help.

You must believe that there is purpose in everyone's life, your life, and a story you can share to have a positive effect on someone else.

If you don't go to the dentist, chances are your teeth may fall out. Same with your mental health; get a check-up.

WARNING: Don't let a bad day with PTSD and depression set you back. Don't let a bad day set you back, period! Expect a bad day now and then to happen, but be prepared or what I like to say, be armed for it. Whatever it is that happens to you mentally or physically, use your mind and fight through it, your mind is powerful. Force yourself to stay active. Feelings of setback are normal. As Shauna mentioned, it's temporary, like a headache, and you will get back to feeling better soon. But you must be willing to stay in the arena and fight back, and that may require some patience and courage.

You will have many challenges in your life, and most of them are unexpected. Accept and take these challenges on, because we can use these challenges to benefit us in the healing process. If you feel you have nowhere to turn, please see the resources at the back of this book. Call someone. Anyone!

Now for some final thoughts that we have already discussed.

We have discussed the beginning, middle, and the end of the lives of first responders and how first responders may be affected by their chosen profession.

We have read the perspectives of first responders and how each one has persevered, not to mention how much each person writing the perspective cares about the first responders who have retired and are still active in the field.

We have discussed how to work through the problems, pain, and panic of the job and life in general and how the Three or Four Ps can haunt you and how they can be fixed.

We have discussed how to fight through things, and that you and I can live wonderful lives with those who care and love us the most.

We have talked about turning points and how to strengthen your mind and body.

We discussed fighting for your life through transformation and being the best version of yourself that you and God intended you to be. "And be not conformed to this world: but be ye transformed by the renewing of your mind, that ye may prove what is that good, and acceptable, and perfect, will of God." Your God.

In this final chapter, we talk about why you must fight.

We fight for ourselves. We fight for our loved ones, and for those who cannot fight for themselves., freedom, peace, love, and happiness. We fight for all people!

Your assignment if you choose to accept it is this: I challenge you!

1) Take a pencil and a piece of paper right now. Write down the reasons why you want to fight, for whom, what you want to fight for, and with whom.

2) Write out your path of how you want to transform your life.

3) Write your goals, values, your core purpose, your affirmations, and keep track of your daily positive habits and get rid of the bad ones. If it helps, look up the definitions for goals, values, core purpose, and affirmations; that may give you some ideas about what applies to you personally.

4) Write your story; it's incredible how good it feels, and we all have a story. Every person that wrote out their perspective for this book had one common theme—we

all felt that it helped us with our healing process, and it took away most of the anger.

5) Most importantly, create an unstoppable mindset to achieve the lifestyle you want to live. Be patient but consistent and know this can take some time.

At the end of our lives, we will only be judged by our relationship with God.

This final thought is for all law enforcement and first responders, active or retired, who need Backup after the Beat.

Don't be blindsided like I was. If sharing my story helps one first responder or one million first responders, or one family member of a first responder, or anyone else, then I'm thankful, and all the tears shed while writing this book were worth it.

I know life scenarios can get you down, but I know, and you know for a fact that you have lived through a million other scenarios in your life, and look, you're still here on this earth. Learn to persevere and move forward and never, never, never quit. People are counting on you. We believe in you.

So, stay in the fight. What's holding you back in life? What's holding you back from winning the fight?

This next paragraph is similar to that found in my last book *Limitless Success*, but if you didn't read that book here it is:

What happens when you finally decide that failure and living an average life is not an option? You can be one decision away from a happy and different life!

What's holding you back? Is it your age? That's only a number.

Your ego? Your pride? What? Do you think you can do it on your own?

Your choices: Okay, maybe you haven't made the best of choices, so learn, repent, pray and just let them go. Start making only good and positive choices.

Is it your past? Just let it go. Your past is behind you. Mistakes? we all make them. Stop making them and just let them go.

Your financial situation: There's more than one way to make money, so take a risk occasionally.

Is it the negative people you surround yourself with? Immediately find new people.

Your own negative thoughts? Then start creating positive ones.

Is it the haters holding you back? Just prove the haters that they are wrong.

Master the transformation.

Stop wasting time being angry. Talk to your loved ones because someday they may leave this earth, and you will not be able to speak with them anymore.

Don't look back on anything and have zero regrets. Move on. Tomorrow is a new day. Start living your life. Fight for what you want.

You can overcome past failures and poor choices and get up every morning and fight like hell to stay in the game. Prioritize what is important and note it down. I bet you will surprise yourself!

Somedays, you will have to suck it up and get back into the fight or struggle one more time, then fail again, then get back into the fight. We have all fallen, but it requires courage to get back up and fight back.

Use your failures as motivation. Use the fear of being average as a motivator.

Fight for your spouses and partners, your children, and family, and become something extraordinary. Make them proud. Continue to do great things. One of my mentors said that we can affect the few, but the few can affect many. My promise to you is that I will never quit fighting, defending, and protecting first responders.

By not giving up and staying in the fight, I've been able to touch and impact lives, especially those of my wife, children, and business partners. If people in my life are not successful, then I'm not successful.

To the police, fire, emergency medical personnel, military, and now COVID-19 survivors, and to all other types of first responders who are reading this book, it is never too late to start your transformation. Live life and start your transformation today! You can do it! We can do it together.

I pray for your happiness and success. I pray that we all can leave a legacy of character. How do you want to be remembered? Write this question down and then write out your answer. Look at your answer frequently.

Take one step at a time; don't let all the stairs in the stairwell intimidate you, stay focused on the first step up, and it will get easier from there. Enjoy your entire life journey because life is not meant to be an internal battlefield.

You may not be where you want to be yet, but get through it and then be grateful you're not where you used to be—and be sure to let the haters know that you made it.

Lord, thank you for never giving up on us! And, for helping me and many others know they're not alone with what they might be going through and knowing that WE'RE NOT CRAZY. Amen

God Bless!

END

Resources

IF YOU ARE IN NEED OF HELP, CALL SOMEONE, CALL ANYONE, PLEASE!

IF YOU OR SOMEONE YOU KNOW IS IN NEED OF HELP, PLEASE REACH OUT IMMEDIATELY!

Here are some resources that could save your life or the life of another.

National Suicide Prevention Lifeline:
The lifeline provides 24/7, free and confidential support for people in distress, prevention and crisis resources for you and your loved ones, and best practices for professionals.
Phone: 1-800-273-TALK (8255), 1-800-SUICIDE (784-2433)
Website: suicidepreventionlifeline.org.
Crisis Text Line: Text "HOME" to 741741
Suicide Prevention Resource Center
Website: www.sprc.org

COPLINE | 1-800-267-5463 – 1-800-COPLINE | copline. org | CopLine is a not-for-profit 501(c)3 dedicated to serving active and retired law enforcement officers and their loved ones by providing CONFIDENTIAL 24/7 trained retired officers for callers who are dealing with various stressors law enforcement careers encounter both on and off the job. Whether it is just a "bad day" or a crisis, they are there to listen and are able to assist with a referral to a culturally competent mental health professional.

Serve & Protect | 615-373-8000 | serveprotect.org | Serve & Protect—mission is to locate and facilitate trauma services for public safety professionals with PTSD symptoms, addictions, or both. Whether residential care or trauma therapists and related services, Serve & Protect works on behalf of the public safety professional to find the right solutions for their real problems.

Thin Line Wellness LLC
Specializes in treating adult PTSD / Trauma related issues.
Contact person: Shauna Shipps (Licensed Professional Counselor)
Phone: 720-753-5710
Fax: 720-770-7296
Email: shauna@thinlinewellness.com
Website: Thinlinewellness.com

CALLFORBACKUP.ORG – In Partnership with Humanizing the Badge, Inc.

Awareness and Prevention/Covid-19 Resilience

For urgent requests: send a text message to (313) 426-2575

IF YOU ARE IN A CRISIS NOW, please contact the National Suicide Prevention Lifeline at 1 (800) 273-TALK (8255) or text the keyword BADGE to 741741 to be connected to a trained crisis counselor, 24/7 – always free and confidential.

Blue H.E.L.P.

Assistance with suicide prevention and honoring the Service of Police Officers who died by suicide.

Email: contact@bluehelp.org

www.1sthelp.net

www.bluehelp.org

Website: www.WEAREBLUEHELP.org

Additional resources are welcomed to be added. Please reach out to Steve Eastin via Facebook.

Bibliography

Shannon, Joel. "At Least 228 Police Officers Died by Suicide in 2019, Blue H.E.L.P. Says. That's More than Were Killed in the Line of Duty." *USA Today*, January 2, 2020. https://www.usatoday.com/story/news/nation/2020/01/02/blue-help-228-police-suicides-2019-highest-total/2799876001/

"CIT & CIP Training." NAMI Greater Milwaukee. Accessed July 29, 2020. https://www.namigrm.org/cit-cip-training

"Mission." Mission | Police - Miami University. Accessed July 29, 2020. https://miamioh.edu/police/about/mission/index.html

"Officer Expectations and Duties." The University of North Carolina at Chapel Hill. Accessed July 29, 2020. https://police.unc.edu/recruitment/officer-expectations-duties/

Brown, Matt. "Don't Say God Is Silent with Your Bible Closed." Desiring God, August 7, 2016. https://www.desiringgod.org/articles/dont-say-god-is-silent-with-your-bible-closed

Buck, Kristan. Web log. *Belles & Bucks* (blog). Kristan Buck, July 18, 2019. https://www.bellesandbucks.com/depression-mindset-matters/

Casting Crowns, "Just Be Held," 2015 , track 7 on *A Live Worship Experience*, Beach Street / Reunion, 2015, compact disc

Guidelines for the management of conditions specifically related to stress. Geneva, Switzerland: World Health Organization; 2013

Morri, Matt. "You Can't Pay Your Bills With Other Peoples Opinions," September 17, 2016. https://www.mattmorris.com/opinions/

"Misquotes and Memes: Did Ben Franklin REALLY Say That?" Newswise. Baylor University, July 1, 2015. https://www.newswise.com/articles/misquotes-and-memes-did-ben-franklin-really-say-that

Index

Made in the USA
Coppell, TX
16 January 2021

48285818R00135